Stop!

The first step is to Register Online & Get Access to:

- Answer Keys & Detailed Explanations
- Additional Math & English Practice
- Weekly Science Quiz
- Reading & Vocabulary Activities
- Summer Diary & Story Competition

Register Now! It's Simple & Fast

Visit: *lumoslearning.com/a/grade2* or Scan the QR code

Enter the Access Code: **SLM26N**

Online Access is Included with your Book Purchase (No extra cost)

Lumos Summer Learning HeadStart - Grade 2 to 3, Student Copy

Contributing Author - Bonnie McRae

Contributing Author - Amber Williams

Contributing Author - Mary Waters Cox

Executive Producer - Mukunda Krishnaswamy

Designer and Illustrator - Sowmya R.

Updated in March 2025

COPYRIGHT ©2019 by Lumos Information Services, LLC. ALL RIGHTS RESERVED. No part of this work covered by the copyright hereon may be reproduced or used in any form or by any means graphic, electronic, or mechanical, including photocopying, recording, taping, Web distribution or information storage and retrieval systems- without the written permission of the publisher.

ISBN 13: 978-1097418343

Printed in the United States of America

FOR SCHOOL EDITION AND PERMISSIONS, CONTACT US

LUMOS INFORMATION SERVICES, LLC

 PO Box 1575, Piscataway, NJ 08855-1575

 www.LumosLearning.com

Email: support@lumoslearning.com

Tel: (732) 384-0146

Fax: (866) 283-6471

Lumos Learning

Step Up Your Skills

WHY SHOULD THIS PROGRAM MATTER TO YOU?

Summer Slide is a significant challenge facing students today. It refers to the decline in academic skills and knowledge that occurs when students are not engaged in educational activities during the summer months.

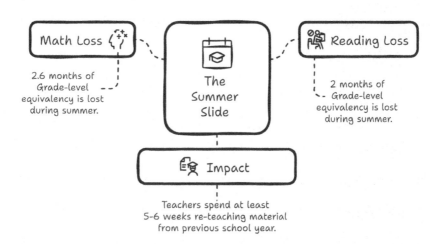

Academic Impact on Students

Math Loss — 2.6 months of Grade-level equivalency is lost during summer.

The Summer Slide

Reading Loss — 2 months of Grade-level equivalency is lost during summer.

Impact — Teachers spend at least 5-6 weeks re-teaching material from previous school year.

How Can You Stay Ahead?

Studies show that students who **practice over the summer retain up to 90%** of their skills, while **those who don't may lose nearly 40%** of what they learned during the school year.

The Lumos Summer Learning HeadStart Program gives you everything you need to stay ahead. It includes:

- **A Printed Workbook** with daily Math and English Practice.
- **An Online Program** with Math, English, Science, Reading, Vocabulary, and Fun Activities.

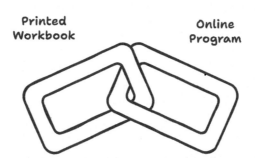

Printed Workbook

Online Program

This blended learning approach ensures you stay on track, gain new skills, and start the school year with confidence. So, start your **Summer Learning HeadStart** today!

TABLE OF CONTENTS

Online Activity   Daily Challenge   Reading   Vocabulary   Science Quiz   Summer Diary

Online Activity   Daily Challenge   Reading   Vocabulary   Science Quiz   Summer Diary

⊕ **Online Activity**   Daily Challenge   Reading   Vocabulary   Science Quiz   Summer Diary

⊕ **Online Activity**   Daily Challenge   Reading   Vocabulary   Science Quiz   Summer Diary

⊕ **Online Activity**

Daily Challenge   Reading   Vocabulary   Science Quiz   Summer Diary

WEEK 1
SUMMER PRACTICE

Solve Addition And Subtraction Problems

1. Linda has 71 pages in her book. She read 23 pages. How many more pages does Linda have left to read?

Ⓐ 52
Ⓑ 94
Ⓒ 58
Ⓓ 48

2. Kim has 24 pieces of candy left after she gave 17 pieces to her classmate. How many pieces of candy did Kim have at first?

Ⓐ 41
Ⓑ 7
Ⓒ 13
Ⓓ 31

3. Lucy had 14 dollars and her father gave her 26. She went and bought an art kit for 15 dollars. How many dollars does Lucy have now?

Ⓐ 40
Ⓑ 25
Ⓒ 9
Ⓓ 55

4. Brad ate 11 grapes from a bag and Jay ate 14 grapes from the same bag. If there are 43 grapes remaining in the bag, how many grapes did the bag originally contain?

Ⓐ 3
Ⓑ 25
Ⓒ 18
Ⓓ 68

Read the story below and answer the questions that follow.

One day, Sara's dad said they were going on a trip to the beach. Sara was happy! She got her things to go. First, she found her bathing suit. She put it on. Then, she went to the bathroom and picked out her best beach towel. Sara put it in her beach bag along with her sunscreen. Her mother told her to hurry up, dad was ready. She didn't want to forget her sand shovel and tools to make a sand castle. She quickly added them to her bag. Sara hurried when she heard her dad start the van.

It was a long drive to the beach. Dad played music on the radio. Mom sang along. Skip, their dog, even whined with the songs. Sara was smiling and having fun. At last, they were there. Dad said to help unload their van. Sara carefully took the picnic basket to the table that her Mom had found by the sand dunes. It was so nice and warm at the beach. Skip ran to the water and jumped in. Dad, Mom and Sara laughed. Mom and Sara got in the water, too. The waves felt funny hitting Sara. She and Mom smiled. Dad was fishing close by. After a bit, Mom said they needed to stop to eat lunch. They ate hot dogs and chips. Skip ate one, too. Then, they rested.

Next, Sara and Dad made a sand castle. Skip laid down on it. That did not stop the fun. Dad said they could all go in one more time. Even Skip joined them. They jumped and swam in the ocean water for a long time. It was getting near dark. They had to leave to go home. Sara and Skip fell asleep on the way back. Everyone had a wonderful time at the beach!

5. Who went to the beach? Mark the correct answer.

Ⓐ Sara went to the beach with her parents.
Ⓑ Sara took her dog, Skip, on a trip to the beach.
Ⓒ Sara went to the beach with friends, Amy and Joan.
Ⓓ Sara, her parents and their dog, Skip, went to the beach.

6. Read the following sentence and question. Choose the best answer.

Dad said they could all go in one more time.
What was he talking about?

Ⓐ The table.
Ⓑ The van.
Ⓒ The water
Ⓓ None of the above.

7. Mark what Sara took to the beach in her bag. Mark all that are correct.

- Ⓐ Dog leash
- Ⓑ Sunscreen
- Ⓒ Sand shovel and tools
- Ⓓ Bathing suit
- Ⓔ Shells
- Ⓕ Purse
- Ⓖ Beach Towel

8. Why do you think they decided to go home? Write your own sentence.

DAY 1

CHALLENGE YOURSELF!

✔ Solve Addition And Subtraction Problems
✔ The Question Session

 www.lumoslearning.com/a/dc2-1

See the first page for Signup details

1. Select TWO equations that equal the same sum.

Ⓐ 12 + 4 = ?
Ⓑ 12 + 2 = ?
Ⓒ 3 + 13 = ?
Ⓓ 4 + 14 = ?

2. Choose TWO equations that equal the same difference.

Ⓐ 19 - 4 = ?
Ⓑ 15 - 8 = ?
Ⓒ 17 - 7 = ?
Ⓓ 20 - 13 = ?

3. Select TWO equations that would equal the same number.

Ⓐ 12 - 8 = ?
Ⓑ 14 - 2 = ?
Ⓒ 9 + 3 = ?
Ⓓ 15 + 3 = ?

4. Select all of the equations that have a sum of 20.

Ⓐ 13 + 7 = ?
Ⓑ 8 + 12 = ?
Ⓒ 1 + 19 = ?
Ⓓ 4 + 6 = ?
Ⓔ 10 + 10 = ?

The Rose Princess
An adaptation of the Rose Princess folk tale

Read the story below and answer the questions that follow.

A long time ago in a faraway kingdom, there lived a beautiful princess. The princess had long red hair. She loved red roses. They called her Princess Rose.

At night-time, she would go out to her balcony. A golden bird would fly to her and sing. She would sing with the bird. The whole village would fall asleep and dream good thoughts.

There was an evil witch who did not like the princess. She cast a spell to turn the princess' hair black.

The next night when the golden bird came and sang, the princess sang again. This time, the village people went to sleep but had bad dreams.

The princess did not know what to do.

She asked the golden bird for help. The bird told her to dip her hair in rose water. The princess did, and it worked.

This made the witch even angrier. She cast a second spell.

This time she got rid of all the roses in the kingdom.

The princess asked the golden bird for help. The bird told her the same thing. The princess could not find any roses.

Just then a prince came with a lock of the princess' hair and dropped it on the ground. It grew into a rose bush full of roses. The princess had rose petals to put in the water and dipped her hair in. Her hair turned red again.

She could once again sing with the golden bird and make the people have good dreams. The princess and prince got married. The evil witch was so upset, she left the kingdom.

They lived happily ever after.

5. Write the sentences in the correct order to retell the story.

- Ⓐ The princess and prince got married and lived happily ever after.
- Ⓑ The princess had long red hair and they called her the Rose Princess.
- Ⓒ The bird told her how to get her red hair back again.
- Ⓓ In the beginning, the princess and bird sang at night and the villagers had good dreams.

6. What is the main meaning behind the folktale?

- Ⓐ There are all kinds of princesses.
- Ⓑ Princesses always marry princes.
- Ⓒ Birds are magical.
- Ⓓ Good wins over evil.

7. Mark the sentence that shows how the prince helped save the day for the princess and villagers.

- Ⓐ Just then a prince came with a lock of the princess' hair and dropped it on the ground.
- Ⓑ Her hair turned red again.
- Ⓒ They lived happily ever after.
- Ⓓ The evil witch was upset.

8. Which sentences do not go with the story? Mark all that apply.

- Ⓐ The bird sang with the princess at night.
- Ⓑ The bird flew away to find the prince.
- Ⓒ The witch was a good witch and loved the princess.
- Ⓓ The prince saved the day

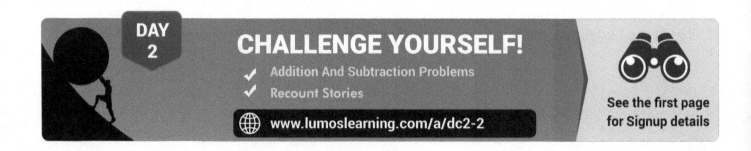

DAY 2

CHALLENGE YOURSELF!

✔ Addition And Subtraction Problems
✔ Recount Stories

🌐 www.lumoslearning.com/a/dc2-2

See the first page
for Signup details

1. Which number below is an even number?

Ⓐ 28
Ⓑ 13
Ⓒ 11
Ⓓ 17

2. Select the equation that equals an even number.

Ⓐ 4+7=?
Ⓑ 3+2=?
Ⓒ 6+6=?
Ⓓ 4+5=?

3. Select the equation that equals an odd number.

Ⓐ 3+3=?
Ⓑ 10+10=?
Ⓒ 4+8=?
Ⓓ 3+6=?

4. James has an odd number of socks in his drawers. Choose the number below that could be the number of socks that James has.

Ⓐ 22
Ⓑ 48
Ⓒ 17
Ⓓ 30

Read the story below and answer the questions that follow.

Javier, Joseph, Wayne and Mike are good friends. They like playing baseball, fishing, hiking, and making model airplanes.

One day the boys wanted to try something new. They had seen the huge kites being flown over the lake. None of them had ever flown a kite.

Javier asked his dad what they needed to do to learn how to fly a kite. His dad told Javier they needed to start with learning how to fly small kites first. They all got their money together and went to the hobby store. Javier and Wayne wanted kites that had dragons on them. Joseph and Mike liked the ones with long tails. The boys agreed on a dragon kite with a long tail.

Now to find the right spot to try it out. Another problem came up. Javier wanted to go to the lake and do it like they had seen the other kites being flown. Wayne said it was ok with him. It was ok with Joseph, too. Mike had a problem with the idea.

He wanted to do it in a park. He said the kite might go into the lake and fall in the water.

The boys talked about it. They made a list of things that could happen at the lake and things that could happen at the park.

The list showed them that the park was the best place. They went to the park. Their dragon kite went up high with its tail flying. They were so happy.

5. What did the boys decide they wanted to learn how to do?

Ⓐ Go surfing
Ⓑ Build a teepee
Ⓒ Fly a kite
Ⓓ Take swimming lessons

6. The boys had 2 problems in the story. What were they?

Ⓐ Where to buy the kite
Ⓑ What kind of kite to buy
Ⓒ Where to fly the kite
Ⓓ How much money to spend

7. How did the boys solve the first problem?

Ⓐ They decided to buy a cat kite.
Ⓑ They decided to buy a kite that had a dragon and had a long tail.
Ⓒ They decided they did not want to buy a kite.
Ⓓ They decided to buy a kite from a different store.

8. How did the boys solve the second problem? Mark the best answer from the story.

Ⓐ They made a list of things that could happen at the lake and things that could happen at the park. The list showed them that the park was the best place. They went to the park. Their dragon kite went up high with its tail flying.

Ⓑ Javier asked his dad what they needed to do to learn how to fly a kite. His dad told Javier they needed to start with learning how to fly small kites first.

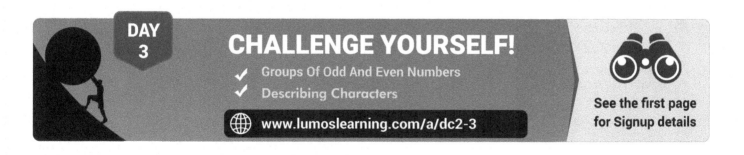

DAY 3

CHALLENGE YOURSELF!
✔ Groups Of Odd And Even Numbers
✔ Describing Characters

🌐 www.lumoslearning.com/a/dc2-3

See the first page for Signup details

1. Choose the addition equation that represents the array.

Ⓐ 3+3+3=?
Ⓑ 5+5+5+5+5=?
Ⓒ 5+5+5=?
Ⓓ 3+5=?

2. Choose the addition equation that represents the array.

Ⓐ 4+4+4+4+4=?
Ⓑ 5+5+5+5+5=?
Ⓒ 5+4=?
Ⓓ 4+4+5+5=?

3. Choose the addition equation that represents the array.

Ⓐ 2+2+6+6+6+6=?
Ⓑ 2+2+2+2+2+2=?
Ⓒ 6+2=?
Ⓓ 6+6+6+6+6+6=?

4. Select the array that equals 12.

Ⓐ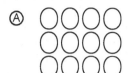

Ⓑ

Ⓒ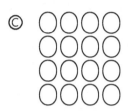

Ⓓ

Going fishing

Read the poem below and answer the questions that follow.

It's a great day to go fishing with Dad.
Get our poles and head to the lake.
Mom says -the bait -don't forget to take!
Spotty, the dog can't go-he's sad.

It's off to the lake, early in the day.
We stop near a shady, cool spot.
That way we won't get too hot.
Poles in the water to wait and hurray!

A bite first off, my pole dipping down.
Pulling and tucking, a keeper for sure!
Oh, no, don't take my lure!
What a big fish to take back to town!
A speckled fish, yellow and brown!

5. How do the rhymes help you better understand the poem? Choose the best answer.

- Ⓐ The rhyming words help by giving meaning to the poem and drawing pictures in your mind to understand it.
- Ⓑ The rhyming words are not helpful.
- Ⓒ The rhyming words make you think of things other than fishing.
- Ⓓ The poem does not have rhyming words in it.

6. What is the rhyming pattern for the first, second and third verses?

- Ⓐ The first, third lines rhyme and the second and fourth lines.
- Ⓑ All lines rhyme in the poem.
- Ⓒ None of the lines rhyme.
- Ⓓ The first, fourth lines rhyme and the second,third lines rhyme.

7. Which words in the poem rhyme with clown? Write them.

8. How can you make the following sentence more vivid? (Alliteration) Choose the best answer.

"A bite first off, my pole dipping down."

Ⓐ A bite, my pole went down.
Ⓑ A bite first off, my pole barely dipping down.
Ⓒ A bite first off, my pole dipping dark deep down.
Ⓓ None of the above.

DAY
4

CHALLENGE YOURSELF!

✔ Addition Using Rectangular Arrays
✔ Figurative Language

 www.lumoslearning.com/a/dc2-4

See the first page
for Signup details

1. Which number has 4 hundreds, 3 ones, and 2 tens?

Ⓐ 432
Ⓑ 234
Ⓒ 423
Ⓓ 342

2. Jake wrote a number with 7 ones, 3 hundreds, and 2 tens. What number did Jake write?

Ⓐ 327
Ⓑ 372
Ⓒ 732
Ⓓ 237

3. Select the number that has 6 tens, 8 ones, and 5 hundreds.

Ⓐ 685
Ⓑ 586
Ⓒ 856
Ⓓ 568

4. Choose a number that does not have any hundreds.

Ⓐ 300
Ⓑ 58
Ⓒ 700
Ⓓ 900

Read the story below and answer the questions that follow.

Chloe was staying at her Nana and Grandpa's house. She loved to help feed the animals. Nana and Grandpa had horses, and chickens.

Every day, Grandpa would ask her to help him with the animals outside. He would feed the horses first. Then he would feed the chickens.

Grandpa was a tall cowboy. He would whistle for the horses to come. The horses would run fast to the fence. Chloe helped him put the horse feed in the buckets and get the hose to fill up the water troughs. She really liked doing that.

When it was time to feed the chickens, Grandpa first looked for eggs in the chicken coop. Then he would make a sound like chickens and put out their feed.

This time, Chloe got to put out the feed. As she was doing that, she heard a "peep, peep, peep" sound. She was very excited. Chloe told her Grandpa, "Grandpa, do you hear that sound? Is it a baby chick?"

Grandpa listened. He laughed and said, "Yes, Chloe. Now where is it ? Let's look."

They looked all around the pen.

Just then, Chloe saw the little yellow chick in a corner of the pen. "Here, Grandpa, here it is!", she shouted.

Grandpa came and slowly picked up the chick. Chloe thought it was so cute.

Grandpa put it in a coop by one of the hens. Soon the hen snuggled the baby chick.

Chloe was so happy! What fun it was to visit and be a help to her Grandpa.

5. How does the start of the story help you to understand the ending? Choose the best answer.

Ⓐ Chloe is at her Nana and Grandpa's house and helps feed the animals outside, where she finds a baby chick.
Ⓑ Chloe feeds the animals outside.
Ⓒ Chloe likes to help.
Ⓓ The start of the story does not help you understand the ending.

6. Put the story sentences in the correct order.

Ⓐ She hears a baby chick when she is feeding the chickens.
Ⓑ Chloe helps Grandpa feed and water the horses.
Ⓒ Chloe is staying at her Nana and Grandpa's house.
Ⓓ Grandpa picks up the baby chick and puts it by a hen.

7. Why is it important that the story begins with where Chloe is? Write your own sentence to answer this question.

8. Which of the following does NOT happen in the story?

   Ⓐ Chloe and Grandpa feed the horses and chickens.
   Ⓑ Chloe hears a baby chick.
   Ⓒ Grandpa will not let Chloe help feed the chicks.
   Ⓓ Grandpa puts the baby chick in a coop by a hen.

DAY 5

CHALLENGE YOURSELF!
   ✓ Three Digit Numbers
   ✓ How is it Written?

🌐 www.lumoslearning.com/a/dc2-5

See the first page for Signup details

LEARN SIGN LANGUAGE

What is American Sign Language?

American Sign Language (ASL) is a complete, complex language that employs signs made by moving the hands combined with facial expressions and postures of the body. It is the primary language of many North Americans who are deaf and is one of several communication options used by people who are deaf or hard-of-hearing.

Where did ASL originate?

The exact beginnings of ASL are not clear, but some suggest that it arose more than 200 years ago from the intermixing of local sign languages and French Sign Language (LSF, or Langue des Signes Française). Today's ASL includes some elements of LSF plus the original local sign languages, which over the years have melded and changed into a rich, complex, and mature language. Modern ASL and modern LSF are distinct languages and, while they still contain some similar signs, can no longer be understood by each other's users

Source: https://www.nidcd.nih.gov/health/american-sign-language

WHY SHOULD ONE LEARN SIGN LANGUAGE?

 ENRICH YOUR COGNITIVE SKILLS
Sign language can enrich the cognitive development of a child. Since, different cognitive skills can be acquired as a child, learning sign language, can be implemented with practice and training in early childhood.

 MAKE NEW FRIENDS
You could communicate better with the hearing-impaired people you meet, if you know the sign language, it is easier to understand and communicate effectively.

 VOLUNTEER
Use your ASL skills to interpret as a volunteer. volunteers can help in making a real difference in people's lives, with their time, effort and commitment.

 BILINGUAL
If you are monolingual, here is an opportunity to become bilingual, with a cause.

 PRIVATE CHAT
It would be useful to converse with a friend or in a group without anyone understanding, what you are up to.

LEARN SIGN LANGUAGE

 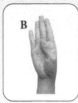 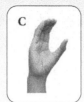 

✔ Sign language is fun if it is practiced with friends

✔ Partner with your friends or family members and try the following activities

ACTIVITY

1. Communicate the following to your friend using the ASL.
   • USA
   • ASL
   If your friend hasn't mastered the ASL yet, give the above alphabet chart to your friend.

2. Try saying your name in ASL using the hand gestures.

3. Have your friend communicate a funny word using ASL and you try to read it without the help of the chart. List the words you tried below.

LET'S LEARN THE NUMBERS

   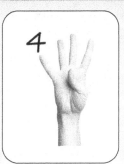 

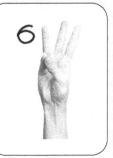    

LET'S LEARN SOME WORDS

RED **ORANGE** **YELLOW** **EAT** **DRINK** **MORE**

GREEN **PURPLE** **BLUE** **PLEASE** **THANK YOU** **SORRY**

WEEK 2
SUMMER PRACTICE

COUNT IN HUNDREDS

1. There are 5 hundreds below. How many tens are there?

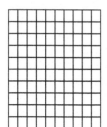 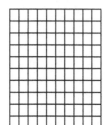 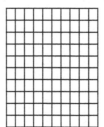 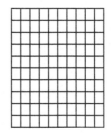 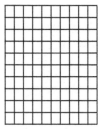

- Ⓐ 50
- Ⓑ 5
- Ⓒ 500
- Ⓓ 55

2. How many groups of 100 are below?

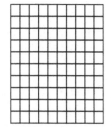 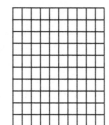 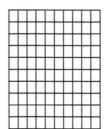

- Ⓐ 30
- Ⓑ 3
- Ⓒ 300
- Ⓓ 33

LumosLearning.com

3. How many ones are shown below?

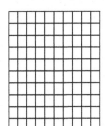 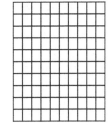

Ⓐ 20
Ⓑ 2
Ⓒ 200
Ⓓ 22

4. Which group shows 400?

 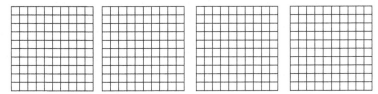

Ⓑ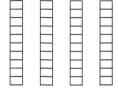

Ⓒ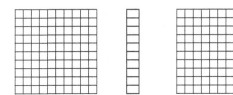

Ⓓ

Read the story below and answer the questions that follow.

Tabitha and Melony had just started ballet classes. The girls had their own ballet shoes and everything. Each Wednesday they went after school to Sally's School of Stars to practice.

"We love Ms. Sally!" Tabitha would say. "She's the best!"

"You got that right!" Melony would reply.

One day at practice, Tabitha took a fall.

"Yikes, my leg hurts!" She yelled.

"Oh, no!" replied Melony. "What happened?"

"Help me, please, get Ms. Sally, NOW!" cried Tabitha.

Melony ran to the front of the class and tugged at Ms. Sally.

"Dear, what is wrong?" asked Ms. Sally.

"HURRY! HURRY! HURRY! Tabitha is hurt BAD!" screamed Melony.

"OH, MY!"

Ms. Sally ran to find Tabitha.

Tabitha sat crying on the floor. "I don't know what happened." She whimpered. "It hurts really awful."

"Go get an ice pack for me, please, Melony. You know where they are, dear. Now, don't worry. I'm calling your mom on my cell, Tabitha." Ms. Sally said this in such a sweet calming voice. Tabitha quit crying when Melony put the ice pack where Ms. Sally said to put it. "Thanks," she said.

In a few minutes, Tabitha's mom came. She carried her to the car.

"Will you call us as soon as you know something, please?" asked Ms. Sally.

"Yes, of course," said Tabitha's mom.

Soon they got the call. It was just a sprained ankle. She would be fine in a few days.

"What a good thing to hear." sighed Ms. Sally.

5. How did Melony know that Tabitha was hurt? Which sentence helps you to know?

Ⓐ "We love Ms. Sally!"
Ⓑ "Thanks," she said.
Ⓒ "I don't know what happened."
Ⓓ "Help me, please, get Ms. Sally, NOW!" cried Tabitha.

6. What point of view (how the girls feel) is shown for Ms. Sally? Write your own sentence. Read the story again for help.

7. Pick two characteristics of Ms. Sally from the story narrative.

- Ⓐ Ms. Sally was a kind and caring person.
- Ⓑ Ms. Sally was not happy with the class.
- Ⓒ Ms. Sally was worried about Tabitha getting hurt.
- Ⓓ Ms. Sally did not listen to Melony.

8. Pretend that you are Melony. How would you say the following sentences?

"HURRY! HURRY! HURRY! Tabitha is hurt BAD!"

- Ⓐ Very loud and with excitement
- Ⓑ Very soft and calm
- Ⓒ A little loud but not too much
- Ⓓ Just read it, not loud or soft

DAY 1

CHALLENGE YOURSELF!

✔ Count In Hundreds
✔ Point of View

🌐 www.lumoslearning.com/a/dc2-6

See the first page
for Signup details

1. What number goes in the blank?
235, 240, 245, 250, ____

Ⓐ 5
Ⓑ 250
Ⓒ 260
Ⓓ 255

2. What is the missing number?
200, ____, 400, 500

Ⓐ 300
Ⓑ 250
Ⓒ 600
Ⓓ 210

3. Start at 67 and count up by tens. What is the 4th number?
67, ___, ____, ____, ____?

Ⓐ 77
Ⓑ 97
Ⓒ 467
Ⓓ 107

4. Select all of the numbers you would say if you were counting by 5's from 0 to 100.

Ⓐ 45
Ⓑ 54
Ⓒ 77
Ⓓ 80
Ⓔ 95

Read the story below and answer the questions that follow.

Mimi was Adelle's grandmother. Adelle liked going to her house in Georgia. Mimi had many things in her huge house. She had teapots, quilts, plates, and spoons.

Spoons were Adelle's favorite. Mimi had them in boxes and special ones hanging on the wall on a rack.

Mimi told stories of her spoons to Adelle.

This was so much fun. Mimi loved spending time with her.

Mimi said, "Adelle, now look at these on the wall. They came from many places. Some are from states here in the U.S. Others are from far away countries I have visited."

Adelle replied, "Tell me, Mimi, tell me all about them."

She began, "Ok, let's see. There are ten spoons on this rack.

The first and last ones are from Finland. They were brought here by my grandmother. The second and sixth ones are from Denmark. We have family there, too. The third one is from Mississippi where I was born. The fourth one is from Texas where you live. The fifth one is just a fun one of Elvis. I loved his songs. The seventh one is from Arkansas, a very pretty place. The eighth one is from Pennsylvania. I went there with your mother once. The ninth one is from an Indian reservation in Oklahoma.

Mimi told me the stories of each of them. She had so many good stories to tell of the places she had been and family members.

5. Who are the characters in this story? List them.

6. Put the spoons in the right order as they appear in the picture (wall rack) and story.

1. Elvis
2. Denmark
3. Oklahoma
4. Arkansas
5. Mississippi
6. Finland
7. Texas
8. Pennsylvania
9. Finland
10. Denmark

7. What kind of relationship do Mimi and Adelle have? Write a sentence.

8. Which answer tells the setting of the story?

Ⓐ Mimi had them in boxes and special ones hanging on the wall on a rack.
Ⓑ Mimi told stories of her spoons to Adelle.
Ⓒ Adelle liked going to her house in Georgia. Mimi had many things in her huge house.
Ⓓ The first and last ones are from Finland.

DAY 2

CHALLENGE YOURSELF!

✔ Count Within 1000
✔ I Can See It!

🌐 www.lumoslearning.com/a/dc2-7

See the first page for Signup details

1. How is 458 written in expanded form?

Ⓐ 400 + 500 + 800
Ⓑ 45 + 8
Ⓒ 400 + 50 + 8
Ⓓ 400 + 58

2. Which number is five hundred thirty?

Ⓐ 503
Ⓑ 530
Ⓒ 533
Ⓓ 513

3. What is 200 + 8 written in standard form?

Ⓐ 280
Ⓑ 288
Ⓒ 208
Ⓓ 2008

4. What is 167 written in word form?

Ⓐ One hundred sixty-seven
Ⓑ One hundred six hundred seven
Ⓒ One hundred six seventy
Ⓓ One hundred sixty

Story #1-Goldilocks and the Three Bears, adaptation version 1

Read the story below and answer the questions that follow.

Once upon a time there were three bears, a papa, a mama and a baby. They were going to eat. Their porridge was too hot to eat, so they went for a walk.

Goldilocks came along and went into their house.

She was hungry and saw the food. Papa Bear's porridge was too hot. Mama Bear's porridge was too cold. Baby Bear's porridge was just right. She ate all of it!

Goldilocks wanted to rest. She saw 3 chairs.

Papa Bear's chair was too hard. Mama Bear's chair was too soft. Baby Bear's chair was just right. But, Goldilocks broke it!

She was tired. Goldilocks saw 3 beds. Papa Bear's bed was too hard. Mama Bear's bed was too soft. Baby Bear's bed was just right. She went fast sleep.

Then, the 3 bears came home. They saw what happened to the porridge, the chair, and Goldilocks in the bed.

The bears roared.

Goldilocks woke up and jumped out a window, running all the way home.

Story #2-Goldilocks, rewritten from memory

Read the story below and answer the questions that follow.

Once upon a time there were three bears who lived in a cottage in the woods. Papa Bear, Mama Bear and Baby Bear. The bears loved a good healthy breakfast. One morning, Mama Bear cooked porridge.

It was too hot to eat, so they went for a walk while it cooled off.

A pretty girl, Goldilocks, had gone into the woods alone. She smelled the food.

She went up to the cottage. No one answered her knock on the door. She went inside.

Here Goldilocks saw three bowls of porridge. She was hungry. She tried the first bowl. It

was too hot.

She tried the second bowl. It was too cold. She tried the third bowl. It was just right. She ate it all!

Then she saw three chairs. She sat in the first chair. It was too hard. She tried the second chair. It was too soft. She sat in the third chair. It was just right, but it broke!

Goldilocks was getting very sleepy after eating all the porridge. She looked for a bed. She found three beds. The first bed was too high and the second was too low. The third bed was just right. She laid down and went to sleep.

The bears got home and saw their porridge. Papa Bear and Mama Bear said, "Someone's been eating my porridge". Baby Bear said, "Someone's been eating my porridge and it's all gone!"

Then they saw their chairs. Papa and Mama Bear said, "Someone's been sitting in my chair." Baby Bear said, "Someone's been sitting in my chair and it's broken!"

Now they decided to take naps. When they saw their beds, Papa Bear and Mama Bear said, "Someone's been sleeping in my bed." Baby Bear said, "Someone's been sleeping in my bed and she's still there

This woke Goldilocks! She was so scared. She ran out of the cottage and all the way home. She said she would never go far away alone again!

5. Why did the bears go for a walk?

Ⓐ They needed to check the forest.
Ⓑ They were doing their exercises.
Ⓒ Their porridge was too hot to eat.
Ⓓ They liked to go for walks.

6. Why did Goldilocks eat the porridge? Write your own sentence.

7. Where did the bears find Goldilocks?

Ⓐ Eating porridge
Ⓑ Walking around the cottage
Ⓒ Asleep in a bed
Ⓓ Sitting in a chair

8. Which sentence best tells about Goldilocks?

Ⓐ A pretty girl, Goldilocks, had gone into the woods alone.
Ⓑ She found three beds.
Ⓒ She sat in the first chair.
Ⓓ The third bed was just right.

DAY 3

CHALLENGE YOURSELF!
✔ Read & Write Numbers To 1000 Using Base-ten Numerals
✔ Alike and Different

🌐 www.lumoslearning.com/a/dc2-8

See the first page for Signup details

1. Choose the symbol that goes in the blank in the number sentence.

458 _____ 485

Ⓐ >
Ⓑ <
Ⓒ =

2. Choose the symbol that goes in the blank in the number sentence.

276 _____ 267

Ⓐ >
Ⓑ <
Ⓒ =

3. Choose the symbol that goes in the blank in the number sentence.

408 _____ 480

Ⓐ >
Ⓑ <
Ⓒ =

4. Choose the comparison that is correct.

Ⓐ 212 > 221
Ⓑ 986 < 968
Ⓒ 521 = 512
Ⓓ 761 > 716

Read the story below and answer the questions that follow.

This is a picture of a Barbeque (BBQ) pit. It is used for cooking many kinds of meat. Some kinds are beef, chicken, turkey, and pork.

They come in different sizes. This one is a large one. Some people use them for cooking during holidays, cook-off contests, big parties, and at restaurants. It can hold a huge amount of meat.

The pit is made of metal. It is a homemade pit. Homemade pits are made by people at their houses. They do not come from a store and are not made in a factory

It is placed on a trailer, so it can be moved around on wheels. This BBQ pit is too heavy to try to move without it being on a trailer.

It has an oven, a temperature gauge, a fire box and a smokestack. It also has a wood rack outside of the pit to place things on such as pans, and cooking utensils. The oven holds the meat on a rack. The temperature gauge shows how hot the oven is cooking. The fire box is where the wood is put and lit to make the heat in the oven. The smokestack is for the smoke to go out while it is cooking.

BBQ pits are very useful to many people.

5. What are some kinds of meat cooked on BBQ pits? Pick the best answer.

Ⓐ Chicken, turkey, and beef
Ⓑ Turkey and chicken
Ⓒ Beef, chicken, turkey and pork
Ⓓ Pork, and beef

6. How is a homemade BBQ pit different from one from a store?

Homemade pits are made by people at their .... They do not come from

a .... and are not made in a ....

7. Why is a big BBQ pit placed on a trailer? Write your own sentence.

8. What is this passage about? Pick the best answer.

  Ⓐ It tells about how to make a BBQ pit.
  Ⓑ It tells the main information about a large BBQ pit.
  Ⓒ It tells about how to cook on a BBQ pit.
  Ⓓ It tells how to heat up a BBQ pit.

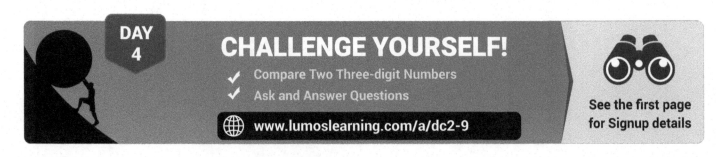

DAY 4

CHALLENGE YOURSELF!
✔ Compare Two Three-digit Numbers
✔ Ask and Answer Questions

🌐 www.lumoslearning.com/a/dc2-9

See the first page
for Signup details

1. ? + 12 = 44

- Ⓐ 56
- Ⓑ 32
- Ⓒ 23
- Ⓓ 65

2. ? − 15 = 62

- Ⓐ 43
- Ⓑ 47
- Ⓒ 57
- Ⓓ 77

3. 21 + ? = 55

- Ⓐ 31
- Ⓑ 34
- Ⓒ 76
- Ⓓ 66

4. Select the equation that does NOT equal 76.

- Ⓐ 99 − 23 = ?
- Ⓑ 40 + 36 = ?
- Ⓒ 2 + 74 = ?
- Ⓓ 100 − 25 = ?

Facts About Tropical Rainforests

Read the story below and answer the questions that follow.

1. Tropical rainforests are homes to many animals and people, and help support our lives. Rainforests are hot, rainy places with lots of huge trees. The plants have many leaves. They are found in places like Central and South America, Africa, Asia and Australia.

2. When scientists talk about rainforests, they talk about the three sections or layers of them. The bottom layer is called the "ground layer". Here live people, animals and plants. The ground is lush and damp. The next layer is the "understory" which is bushy. You can find trees and animals in this layer, too. The top is called the "canopy". It is very thick. Very little light gets in, so the rainforest is dark. The canopy is the protection for the rainforest.

3. If you look down from an airplane on a rainforest it looks like a big green carpet or green grass everywhere. The plants from the rainforests help the world to breathe. They make oxygen for us. We need this to breathe.

4. Many animals and insects live in rainforests on the bottom, understory or canopy levels. There are monkeys, parrots, toucans, birds, jaguars, snakes, butterflies, frogs, anteaters, and ants.

5. Beautiful plants live there, too. Flowers like the hibiscus, orchid, and passion flower thrive in rainforests.

6. The rainforests are home to lakes, streams, and rivers. Here live other creatures like crocodiles, water lizards, turtles, snakes, and fish.

7. People in tribes have called the rainforests their home for centuries. They can find most everything they need to live on right in the rainforests.

8. Groups are helping to keep the rainforests alive for the people and animals there and for us to keep fresh air on earth.

5. What is the main topic of this article?

Ⓐ The article is about crocodiles.
Ⓑ The article is about tribes in rainforests.
Ⓒ The article is about how people are helping the rainforests.
Ⓓ The article gives facts about rainforests.

6. Fill in the blank to show the main topic.

.... are homes to many animals, people, and help support our lives.

7. List the types of flowers in paragraph 5.

8. Fill in the chart with details from paragraph 4 and 6.

	Lives in water or on land	Land
snakes	☐	☐
monkeys	☐	☐
jaguars	☐	☐
parrots	☐	☐

DAY 5

CHALLENGE YOURSELF!

✔ Add And Subtract Within 100 Using Place Values
✔ The Main Idea

 www.lumoslearning.com/a/dc2-10

See the first page
for Signup details

7 SIMPLE WAYS TO IMPROVE YOUR ROAD SKATING

There is no better feeling than the freedom you feel from Road Skating. It is unlike anything else. The wind through your hair as you glide down the road on a beautiful sunny day. The breeze keeping you cool while you enjoy yourself. It is truly a magical feeling. Like anything else in life, you want to have fun while improving and be careful when you are playing. Here are seven simple ways to improve on your road skating.

1. Choosing the perfect skates for you

Before you can get out there and start skating, you need to decide what type of skates you want to wear. There are two different types of skates you can choose from. The first type of skates are called inline skates. These have four wheels together in a straight line, going down the middle, from the front to the back of the skate. They look similar to ice skates, but are for using outdoors or on a hardwood surface. Inline skates are the more common of the two yet are a little harder to learn to use.

The second type of skates are called quad skates. Quads have two wheels in the front and two wheels in the back. Most quads will have a stopper in the front by the toe. This allows skaters to stop quicker and easier. Inline skates usually don't have a stopper, but there are some that do have one at the back of the skate.

Both skates have their strengths and weaknesses. Each type of skate has a unique feel to the way you skate in them. Some people don't like inlines because of the lack of feeling safe, others believe they are safer than skating with quads. You should try the two styles out and see what feels more natural for you.

2. Dress appropriately

It is important to dress appropriately. It seems like something you automatically do, but it is just as important as anything else. If it's a cool breezy day you might want to wear windbreaker pants and a t-shirt. On hot days, shorts would be a better dress option. Wearing a hat or sunglasses is useful in keeping the sun out of your eyes. Preparing an outfit for the day will help keep you cool outside.

3. Check the weather for the day

Weather will be a factor in deciding when to go out. It doesn't just factor in to how you dress. It also will determine if that day is good to skate at all. A beautiful day will bring hours of fun, but bad weather is never good. If there is in climate weather in the forecast then it may be a good idea to hold off on skating. Don't get caught in the rain because you forgot to check.

4. Safety first when skating

Safely skating is a good way to make sure that you can have a great time without any serious injuries. You should never go out without proper safety equipment. When getting ready, check and make sure you have everything you need. First thing you will need is a helmet. Helmets are a cool way to express yourself and keep your head safe. Helmets come in a variety of styles and colors, and can be a way to show your unique personality to everyone else around you.

Elbow pads and knee pads are also necessary when getting ready. When we are Road Skating we will fall from time to time. It happens to everyone and is just part of skating. Elbow pads and knee pads will help keep you unharmed whenever this happens. They keep us from getting scraped up, which doesn't feel so good. Wrist guards should be worn as well. Naturally, when we fall, we put our hands down to stop us. Wrist guards help protect your wrists from getting damaged when this happens.

LumosLearning.com

5. Practice makes perfect: don't be scared to fail

Like anything in life, the more you practice something the easier it will come to you. It takes time and effort to become better at anything you do. We evolve everyday as we continue to strive to get better. Failure is something we have to deal with whenever working towards our goals. If everything in life comes easily then there would be no competitive spirit. The drive to be better makes things in life worth working towards. It is good to be scared sometimes. Fear brings out the best in you, but don't let it overwhelm you. If you fall, get back up and try again. In the moment it may seem pointless to continue, but the outcome will be rewarding.

6. Don't skate on an empty stomach and keep hydrated

Skating takes a lot of energy. Eating a good meal is very important when planning a day of roller exercise. Give yourself at least a half hour to digest your food before going out. Water is key too. Staying hydrated will keep you going throughout the day. It is important to have plenty of water ready as needed. Water and a good meal are essential.

7. Have fun while skating

Skating is meant to be fun. You should be able to be yourself and not worry about being judged by others. Just remember, if it wasn't fun then you probably wouldn't want to be doing it. Having fun while skating will make all that practice seem less like practice and more like an activity.

Following these simple guidelines will help you become a better skater. You will get better the more you practice, and having fun while doing it will make you want to practice more often. Everything will fall into place if you let it. Remember, we earn everything we get so how you go about getting there will determine the success you have in your attempts.

WEEK 3
SUMMER PRACTICE

ADD FOUR TWO-DIGIT NUMBERS

1. Choose the correct sum for the equation
   $10 + 45 + 10 + 20 = ?$

   Ⓐ 75
   Ⓑ 85
   Ⓒ 55
   Ⓓ 80

2. Choose the correct sum for the equation
   $15 + 15 + 20 + 30 = ?$

   Ⓐ 80
   Ⓑ 30
   Ⓒ 50
   Ⓓ 75

3. Drew scored 12 points in the first game, 10 points in the second game, 16 points in the third game, and 8 points in the fourth game. How many total points did Drew score in all four games ?

   Ⓐ 26
   Ⓑ 12
   Ⓒ 22
   Ⓓ 46

4. What is the sum of 28, 31, 5, and 19?

   Ⓐ 84
   Ⓑ 48
   Ⓒ 83
   Ⓓ 78

Read the story below and answer the questions that follow.

George Washington was the first President of the United States. There are many events that led to this happening. He was born in Virginia on February 22, 1732.

Our country was ruled by England.

George became a surveyor. This means that he did things like making maps.

He was also a farmer. His farm was called Mount Vernon.

George Washington married Martha Custis. She already had 2 children. He helped raise them.

People did not want to be a part of England. They wanted their own country. He joined these people. George was a general in the American Revolutionary Army.

He fought in the Revolutionary War to free America from England.
It was a long and hard fight. The colonists won the war.

The new country was named the United States of America.

George Washington was elected as the first President in 1789. He was a good man and very important person in the history of our country.

5. How did George Washington help our country? Pick 2 answers.

- Ⓐ He became a surveyor
- Ⓑ He fought in the American Revolutionary War
- Ⓒ He got married.
- Ⓓ He became the first President of the United States.

6. Who ruled America when George was born? Fill in the blank.

.... ruled America at that time.

7. Put the events in the right order to show how one led to another.

Ⓐ George Washington was important to our country.
Ⓑ George Washington joined the people in a war against England.
Ⓒ He was a general in the American Revolutionary War.
Ⓓ George Washington became President of the United States

8. Which of the sentences does NOT show how George Washington helped our country?

Ⓐ He lived on a farm named Mount Vernon.
Ⓑ He was important to our country.
Ⓒ He joined the fight against England.
Ⓓ He was President of the United States.

DAY 1

CHALLENGE YOURSELF!
✔ Add Four Two-digit Numbers
✔ Connect The Dots

www.lumoslearning.com/a/dc2-11

See the first page
for Signup details

1. Solve: 763 − 211 = ?

Ⓐ 974
Ⓑ 551
Ⓒ 972
Ⓓ 552

2. Solve: 287 + 109 = ?

Ⓐ 396
Ⓑ 386
Ⓒ 392
Ⓓ 178

3. What is the sum of 418 and 220?

Ⓐ 198
Ⓑ 218
Ⓒ 638
Ⓓ 538

4. What is the difference between 733 and 190?

Ⓐ 543
Ⓑ 923
Ⓒ 663
Ⓓ 823

Read and answer the questions.

Have you ever heard the wind blowing? Have you looked up in the trees and seen the leaves moving? When air is moved around outside it is called wind. The wind can be stronger than the branches of a tree. Wind can <u>bend</u> the branches up and down and break trees. High winds can be dangerous to people and things. You can even hear wind howling as it moves from one area to another.

5. What is moving air called?

6. What does bend mean in the text?

Ⓐ to run around
Ⓑ to move one way or another
Ⓒ to fix
Ⓓ to change color

Sound

Sound can travel. Sound must have material to go through like air, or water. When sound goes through air it is not as fast as if it goes through water. Sound moves 4 times quicker through water. How fast? Scientists say that sound can go about 767miles an hour when it travels in water.

7. Which two words mean the same in the text? Pick two sets of words.

Ⓐ sound, material
Ⓑ fast, quicker
Ⓒ goes, moves
Ⓓ say, can

8. What examples of material are given in discussing sound?

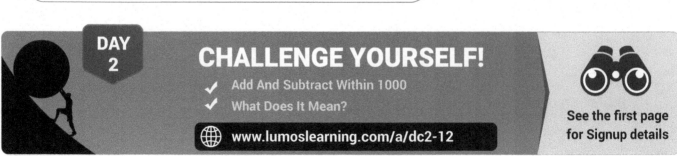

DAY
2
CHALLENGE YOURSELF!
✓ Add And Subtract Within 1000
✓ What Does It Mean?
🌐 www.lumoslearning.com/a/dc2-12

See the first page
for Signup details

1. What number is 10 more than 458?

- (A) 558
- (B) 448
- (C) 468
- (D) 358

2. What is 100 less than 450?

- (A) 350
- (B) 550
- (C) 340
- (D) 540

3. 678 is 10 less than what number?

- (A) 778
- (B) 578
- (C) 668
- (D) 688

4. 743 is 100 more than what number?

- (A) 753
- (B) 843
- (C) 643
- (D) 733

Read the story below and answer the questions that follow.

Citizen- a person living in a community.
Community - the area in which people live.
Congestion - blocked or slowed.
Rural - a farm or country community.
Store - a place where you buy things you need to live on or want.
Suburb - a community close by a city.
Transportation - ways to get from one place to another such as by bus, car, truck, subway, bicycle, train, or plane.
Urban - a city community where many businesses are located.

Citizens of communities do different things in their daily lives. The people in the urban community travel by many kinds of transportation. They often go from one area of the city to others. Some may take cars and then subways to work. Others hop on buses from their locations.

Those who live in the suburbs may find it more difficult to get into the city. Their time can be taken up by congestion on the freeways or searching for parking downtown. This might make them arrive late for work or meetings. Rural citizens may not go into the city very often. They might raise their own goods. Farming and ranching are a part of their lives. There are some small stores in these areas. When rural citizens go to urban or suburban areas it will take them much longer to get there. They may have trouble finding their way around as urban communities may change. Most citizens of rural areas like living where there are no large businesses around them. They enjoy the peace and quiet of rural life.

Those living in urban and suburban communities have large stores or malls to go to when buying what they want or need. People living in different communities have different ways of living their daily lives.

5. Match the vocabulary words with their definitions.

	Country living	City living	Close to the city living
Urban	☐	☐	☐
Rural	☐	☐	☐
Suburban	☐	☐	☐

6. Using the glossary to help you, why would congestion be a problem for those in the suburbs?

Ⓐ Congestion would be a problem because it might make them late for their jobs.
Ⓑ Congestion would not be a problem because it would help them get to work faster
Ⓒ Congestion would be a problem because they could not stop when they wanted to.
Ⓓ Congestion would make it easier for them to listen to the radio.

7. List the forms of transportation found in the glossary.

8. Tell what a citizen is?

DAY 3

CHALLENGE YOURSELF!

✔ Mental Addition And Subtraction In Steps Of 10
✔ Special Text Parts

🌐 www.lumoslearning.com/a/dc2-13

See the first page for Signup details

1. What is another way to add 43 + 16?

Ⓐ (40 + 10) + (3 + 6)
Ⓑ (40 + 1) + (30 + 6)
Ⓒ (34) + (61)
Ⓓ (4 + 1) + (30 + 60)

2. What is another way to add 27 + 12?

Ⓐ (20 + 70) + (1 + 2)
Ⓑ (20 + 10) + (7 + 2)
Ⓒ (71 + 22)
Ⓓ (72 + 21)

3. What is another way to add 31 + 67?

Ⓐ (60 + 30) + (1 + 7)
Ⓑ (6 + 3) + (70 + 40)
Ⓒ (30 + 6) + (40 + 7)
Ⓓ (43 + 76)

4. (40 + 10) + (6 + 5) could be another way to add which equation below?

Ⓐ 64 + 51 = ?
Ⓑ 14 + 9 = ?
Ⓒ 46 + 15 = ?
Ⓓ 406 + 105 = ?

Read the story below and answer the questions that follow.

Owls are beautiful! Let's look at their characteristics.

Owls live in many places. Some live in rainforests, deserts, farms, marshes, woods, and on plains.

Owls can be seen in other places, too. The Snowy Owl and Hark Owl can stay in very cold weather.

They do not like the hot or wet weather.

Owls can make very loud noises. People know that owls can "hoot". Owls can make different sounds. They can shriek, hoot, bark, and even grunt like a pig. If they are upset, the noise can sound like clicking and hissing. Get away if you hear this sound when you are near an owl.

Most owls come out at night. They are nocturnal.

Owls have good eyes and even better hearing. They do not have a sense of smell.

Owls like to eat small prey. Owls fly then swoop down and pick their food up with their claws or beaks. They eat insects, snakes, mice, birds, squirrels, and rabbits depending on the kind of owl.

People have owls for pets, too. It is not easy to have a pet owl. You would need to read up on where to find owls to buy, what to keep them in, how to feed them and train them.

Owls are very interesting and beautiful birds.

---

5. What is the main idea of this passage?

Ⓐ Owls are nocturnal.
Ⓑ Owls have many characteristics.
Ⓒ Some people have owls as pets.
Ⓓ Owls have good hearing.

---

6. Fill in the chart to show the characteristics of owls. Mark yes or no.

	Yes	No
Nocturnal	○	○
Can be pets	○	○
Have good sense of smell	○	○
Can make loud noises	○	○

7. What is another word for "characteristic"? Read the words and definitions below and choose one.

Ⓐ Shrieking – loud noises, screaming, yelling
Ⓑ Trait - quality that makes something what it is, sets it apart from other things
Ⓒ Nocturnal- comes out at night, sleeps during the day
Ⓓ Swoops- dives down in a fast way

8. Think about the main idea. Pick two answers that are true about owls.

Ⓐ Owls usually come out in daylight.
Ⓑ Owls might sleep during the day.
Ⓒ Owls fly down to get their food.
Ⓓ Owls are not good at seeing or hearing.

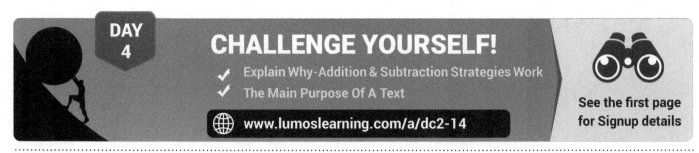

DAY 4

CHALLENGE YOURSELF!
✔ Explain Why-Addition & Subtraction Strategies Work
✔ The Main Purpose Of A Text

🌐 www.lumoslearning.com/a/dc2-14

See the first page for Signup details

1. What number is represented below?

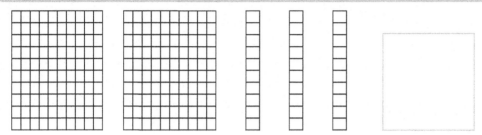

- Ⓐ 213
- Ⓑ 321
- Ⓒ 231
- Ⓓ 132

2. What number is 9 ones, 3 tens, 8 hundreds?

- Ⓐ 938
- Ⓑ 389
- Ⓒ 839
- Ⓓ 398

3. Which choice below is the same as 419?

- Ⓐ 1 hundred, 4 tens, 9 ones
- Ⓑ 9 ones, 4 hundreds, 1 ten
- Ⓒ 4 ones, 1 ten, 9 hundreds
- Ⓓ 1 hundred, 9 tens, 1 one

4. How many hundreds can be taken from 88 tens?

- Ⓐ 80
- Ⓑ 8
- Ⓒ 88
- Ⓓ 800

The Pulley - A Simple Machine

Read the passage below and answer the questions that follow.

A blind in a room

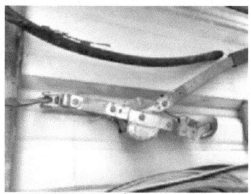
A come-along

A fishing pole

There are many kinds of simple machines. Simple machines make work easier. Pulleys are a kind of simple machine. They can be found in many things we use or see every day. Simple machines do not have a lot of parts. Pulleys are important in making work easier.

Look at the pictures. They all use pulleys. Pulleys come in many sizes. The size depends on the job to be done.

A pulley is a wheel. It is used with a rope, cord, belt or chain. If you pull on the rope, the other end goes up. Pulleys can make things go up and down and pull things. A flagpole runs on a pully. Construction cranes have pulleys. Have you ever seen someone raise a blind to see outside of a window? The blind runs on a pulley. The pictures show a blind in a room, a come-along, and a fishing pole. They all have pulleys.

Each type of pulley has a way to help make the job easier. The string on the blind is connected to the pulley and can raise or lower the blind. The come-along can be attached to a heavy object. By cranking the come-along, the pulley will move the object for you. With a fishing pole, the pulley helps to bring in the fishing line to make it easier to pull in the fish you catch.

Jobs and tasks would be much harder without the use of pulleys. Pulleys help people in many ways.

5. How do the pictures of objects using pulleys help you to understand the text?

Ⓐ The pictures along with the text do not help you at all.
Ⓑ The pictures along with the text show the pulleys working.
Ⓒ The pictures along with the text show you how to take apart pulleys.
Ⓓ The pictures along with the text give you a better understanding of how pulleys work in things.

6. What part of this text helps to clarify the meaning? Mark the best answer.

Ⓐ Pulleys are a kind of simple machine.
Ⓑ They can be found in many things we use or see every day.
Ⓒ Simple machines do not have a lot of parts.
Ⓓ Pulleys are important in making work easier.

7. Match the types of pulleys in the objects to their meaning.

	Helps to bring in your fish	Helps to raise or lower to see outside	Helps to move heavy objects
Blinds	○	○	○
Come-along	○	○	○
Fishing pole	○	○	○

8. How do the pictures help you? Write your own sentence.

DAY 5

CHALLENGE YOURSELF!
✔ Bundle Of Tens
✔ Informational Illustration

🌐 www.lumoslearning.com/a/dc2-15

See the first page for Signup details

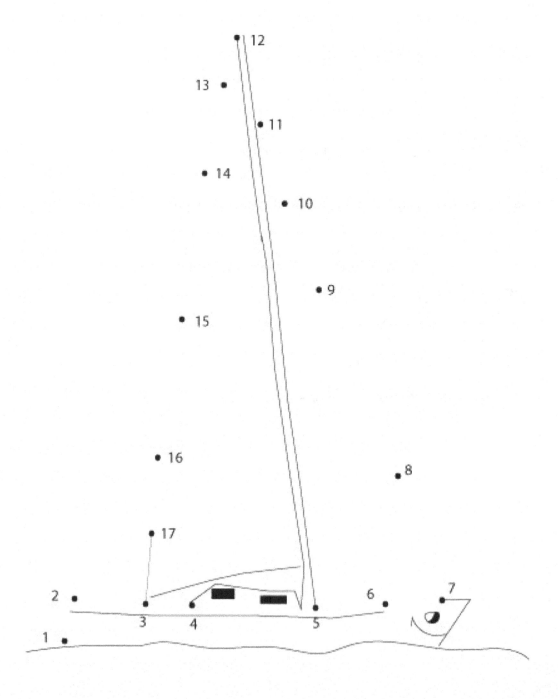

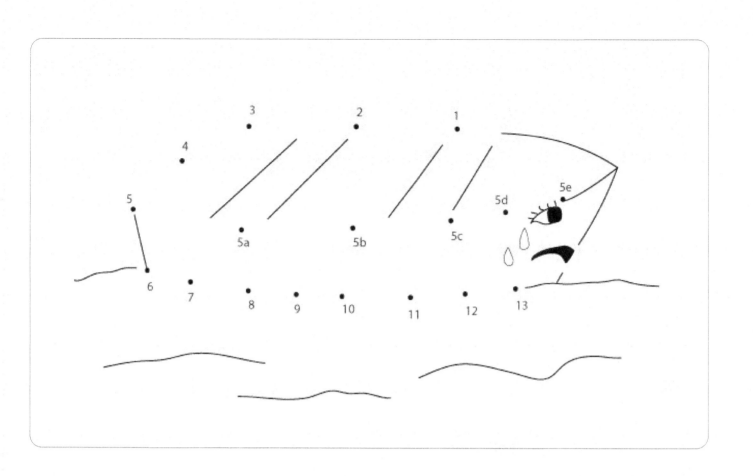

WEEK 4
SUMMER PRACTICE

1. How many inches long is the line below?

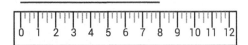

Ⓐ 8 inches
Ⓑ 18 inches
Ⓒ 80 inches
Ⓓ 1/8 inches

2. How many inches long is the line?

Ⓐ 9 inches
Ⓑ 2 inches
Ⓒ 7 inches
Ⓓ 12 inches

3. How many inches long is the line?

Ⓐ   3 inches
Ⓑ   12 inches
Ⓒ   9 inches
Ⓓ   36 inches

4. Brad cut a piece of string that is 4 inches. What choice below can represent Brad's string?

Ⓐ

Ⓑ

Ⓒ

Ⓓ

Look at the pictures. Read the text and answer the questions. Reread the text to help you.

Signs to help people

You can see signs everywhere you go. Signs show and tell you about things and places. If you are on a trip, a sign might tell you how far the next town is or where an attraction is located. While in a town or on a street, you see signs for names of stores, businesses, and streets. You need to know that many signs tell us things to do and remember for our safety.

Some signs you know quickly. When you are riding in a car with your parents or others, you might see the stop sign. It is easily recognized. The word stop is in bold and the sign background is red. If you see this sign, be sure to stop. If you are walking look both ways to check to see if anything is coming before you go on.

Another sign that is important in traveling is the buckle up seat belt sign. Many states have this on their highways to remind people that not only it is the law to buckle up, but it is for safety, too. Seat belts keep you from getting hurt in case you are in an accident. Buckle up every time you get in a vehicle.

The third sign shown you might not notice, but it is very important whether you are walking along with a friend or riding in a vehicle. If you see the DANGER sign, it means that you must not go near that place. It might mean that the place or building has chemicals or materials that are harmful. You need to stay away because there is a threat that you could be hurt.

Signs are important in our lives and can help us know where to go, what to do, and what to stay away from, too.

5. What point is the author trying to make in this selection? Mark the best answer.

Ⓐ The point the author is trying to make is that signs are everywhere.
Ⓑ The point the author is trying to make is that signs are important to learn and follow.
Ⓒ The point the author is trying to make is to buckle up.
Ⓓ The point the author is trying to make is that signs are on streets.

6. Fill in the T-chart to show what the reasons are that support the point of the text.

	Danger signs tell you to stay away from something.	Seat belt signs tell you to put on your seat belt.	Stop signs tell you to stop.
Stop Sign	☐	☐	☐
Buckle up sign.	☐	☐	☐
Danger Sign	☐	☐	☐

7. Which 2 are NOT reasons for following signs?

Ⓐ Signs are hard to figure out.
Ⓑ Only adults need to learn signs.
Ⓒ Signs help keep you safe.
Ⓓ Signs show you what to and what not to do.

8. Using the author's point and reasons, write why signs are important. Reread the text for help

DAY 1

CHALLENGE YOURSELF!

✔ Measuring Length Of Objects
✔ Reason it out

🌐 www.lumoslearning.com/a/dc2-16

See the first page for Signup details

1. Look at the ruler below, then choose the true statement.

Ⓐ 2 inches is equivalent to 2 centimeters.
Ⓑ Inches are shorter than centimeters.
Ⓒ 7 centimeters is less than 3 inches.
Ⓓ 12 centimeters is closer to 6 inches than 5 inches.

2. Look at the ruler below, then choose the true statement.

Ⓐ 3 inches is between 7 and 8 centimeters.
Ⓑ There are 12 centimeters in 4 inches.
Ⓒ 8 centimeters is less than 3 inches.
Ⓓ 5 inches is longer than 13 centimeters.

3. Look at the ruler below, then choose the statement that is NOT true.

Ⓐ 1 inch is between 2 and 3 centimeters.
Ⓑ 7 centimeters is less than 3 inches.
Ⓒ 10 centimeters are less than 4 inches.
Ⓓ 2 ½ inches is more than 7 centimeters.

4. Look at the ruler below, then choose the statement that is NOT true.

Ⓐ 1 centimeter is less than ½ an inch.
Ⓑ 7 centimeters is closer to 2 inches than 3 inches.
Ⓒ 5 inches is less than 13 centimeters.
Ⓓ 2 inches is closer to 5 centimeters than 6 centimeters.

Read the Informational text below and answer the questions that follow.

Do You Know Cats?

Cats are very interesting! Many people have them as pets.

Here are a few neat facts you might not know about cats.

1. Cats like to sleep most of the time. (about 12 hours a day)
2. They can jump up to 7x as long as they are.
3. Their tongues are like sandpaper.
4. Cats can make over 100 different kinds of noises.
5. When put their paws in and out, they are happy.
6. A grown-up cat has 30 teeth.
7. They can jump from high places and still be ok.
8. They say hello to other cats by touching noses.
9. They cannot see if it is totally dark.
10. Cats can run very fast.
11. Their sense of hearing is excellent.
12. Calico cats are usually girl cats.
13. Baby cats are called kittens, grown boy cats are called Toms, and grown girl cats can be called Queens.

Cat Facts

I read an article on important things we need to know about cats. Here are some of those things.

1. Cats can be sad.
2. Cats cannot see in the dark like some people think. They need to have a little bit of light to see
3. Cats can hear very well, but not as good as dogs.
4. They have 20 bones in their tails.
5. Cats say hi to each other by touching their noses to each other.
6. Cats can be right or left handed. Most cats do use their right paw more.
7. Cats that live with people usually live to be 12 yrs old.
8. Cats take baths by licking themselves.
9. Domestic cats (those that live with people) love to play.
10. There are about 500 kinds of domestic cats.
11. Kittens are born with blue eyes and then most change colors.
12. Cats have 4 legs, 5 toes on each front paw, only 4 on back paws.
13. They sleep most of the day.

5. What does this article talk mostly about? Mark the best answer that supports it.

Ⓐ Cats sleep most of the time.
Ⓑ Calico cats are usually girl cats.
Ⓒ There are many interesting facts about cats.
Ⓓ Cats can jump high.

6. What sense of hearing do cats have? Mark the best answer.

Ⓐ Their sense of hearing is 7x better than ours.
Ⓑ They have a very good sense of hearing.
Ⓒ They cannot hear very well.
Ⓓ It does not tell about their sense of hearing.

7. List the different names the text says cats can be called.

8. Are cats left or right handed? Write your own sentence. Use a fact from the list to help you.

DAY 2

CHALLENGE YOURSELF!

✔ Measure Length Of Object Using Two Different Length Units
✔ Compare And Contrast

 www.lumoslearning.com/a/dc2-17

See the first page
for Signup details

1. The height of an orange is about 8 ___?

Ⓐ Centimeters
Ⓑ Feet
Ⓒ Inches
Ⓓ Meters

2. The length of a fork is about 6 _____ ?

Ⓐ Centimeters
Ⓑ Feet
Ⓒ Inches
Ⓓ Meters

3. The height of a door is about 7 ___?

Ⓐ Centimeters
Ⓑ Feet
Ⓒ Inches
Ⓓ Meters

4. The length of a paper clip is about 12 ___?

Ⓐ Centimeters
Ⓑ Feet
Ⓒ Inches
Ⓓ Meters

5. Read the list of words below. When we look at words, we can put them in order of the alphabet to help understand and read them. This list can be done by the first letter. Write the words in the correct ABC order.

Ⓐ banana	1
Ⓑ drive	2
Ⓒ apple	3
Ⓓ carrot	4
Ⓔ elephant	5

6. We can also sort words by their second letter if the first letter is the same. Look at the list below. Mark the long vowel word that is NOT in the correct ABC order.

Ⓐ Tail
Ⓑ Train
Ⓒ Team
Ⓓ Tone

7. When 2 vowels are together in a word, the first vowel is usually long and the second one silent. Read the list of words in the box and mark which has a short vowel sound, and which has a long vowel sound

	Short vowel sound	Long vowel sound
Mail	☐	☐
Street	☐	☐
Bat	☐	☐
Box	☐	☐

8. Read the words below and write the vowel combination for each.

	Vowel Combination
sneak	
goat	
trail	
clean	
deep	

DAY 3

CHALLENGE YOURSELF!
✔ Estimate Lengths Using Different Units Of Measurement
✔ Decode The Words

 www.lumoslearning.com/a/dc2-18

See the first page
for Signup details

1. How much longer is Rectangle A than Rectangle B?

Rectangle A

Rectangle B

(A) 3 ½ inches
(B) 4 centimeters
(C) 4 inches
(D) 3 ½ centimeters

2. How much shorter is Rectangle A than Rectangle B?

Rectangle A

Rectangle B

(A) 10 ½ centimeters
(B) 10 centimeters
(C) 10 inches
(D) 10 ½ inches

3. How much longer is Rectangle B than Rectangle A?

Rectangle A

Rectangle B

(A) The rectangles are the same length.
(B) 3 centimeters
(C) 5 centimeters
(D) 2 centimeters

4. How much longer is Rectangle A than Rectangle B?

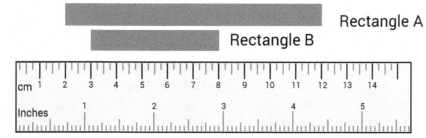

Ⓐ   5 centimeters
Ⓑ   4 centimeters
Ⓒ   3 inches
Ⓓ   12 inches

Read the Informational text below and answer the questions that follow.

A giraffe is a very tall animal. They can be found in the wild in Africa. Many zoos have giraffes, too. When we think of or picture a giraffe, we see the long, long neck. They are extremely tall. It would take at about 3 humans to be as tall as a giraffe. By being this tall, they can keep a close eye out for any animals that could hurt them, like hyenas or lions.

They weigh over 2 thousand pounds and can run about 35 miles an hour.
A funny thing is that the male is called a bull and the female is called a cow.

Giraffes are plant eating animals. They eat leaves and tiny branches called twigs. Giraffes do not drink much water. The reason for this is that they get most of their water from the leaves they eat. 75% of the time, giraffes are eating or roaming around. They even sleep standing up.

5. Which 3 of the following are facts about giraffes that you read in the story?

Ⓐ Giraffes weigh over 2 thousand pounds.
Ⓑ Giraffes sleep most of the day.
Ⓒ Giraffes sleep standing up.
Ⓓ Giraffes can be found in the wild in Africa.

6. Find the correct sentence about how fast giraffes can run. Mark your answer.

Ⓐ They can run over 75 miles an hour
Ⓑ They can run about 35 miles an hour.
Ⓒ They do not run, they jump.
Ⓓ They run about 10 miles an hour.

7. Why don't giraffes drink a lot of water like other animals? Write your own sentence.

8. Look at the chart. Mark if the detail is or is not a fact about giraffes.

	Is a fact	Is not a fact
Giraffes eat mice.	☐	☐
Giraffes can be 3 times taller than people.	☐	☐
Giraffes are only found in Africa.	☐	☐
Males are called bulls and females are called cows.	☐	☐

DAY 4

CHALLENGE YOURSELF!
✔ Compare The Length Of Objects
✔ Comprehend The Text

 www.lumoslearning.com/a/dc2-19

See the first page
for Signup details

1. Brian had a piece of string that measures 36 inches. He cut the string and now the string is 12 inches. How much string did Brian cut?

Ⓐ 12 inches
Ⓑ 36 inches
Ⓒ 24 inches
Ⓓ 48 inches

2. The hallway from the cafeteria door to the office door is about 65 feet. From the office door to the gym door is about 30 feet. About how many feet is it from the cafeteria door to the gym door?

Ⓐ About 95 feet
Ⓑ About 30 feet
Ⓒ About 35 feet
Ⓓ About 65 feet

3. Lola cut 3 pieces of string all the same length in inches. The total length of all 3 pieces of string is 12 inches combined. What is the length of each piece of string?

Ⓐ 12 inches
Ⓑ 6 inches
Ⓒ 3 inches
Ⓓ 4 inches

4. Trevor's ink pen is 4 inches long. If he has 5 ink pens, what is the total length of all the pens if they were lined up?

Ⓐ 9 inches
Ⓑ 16 inches
Ⓒ 20 inches
Ⓓ 25 inches

Read the Informational text below and answer the questions that follow.

Did you know that Benjamin Franklin was not only an inventor, but a scientist, soldier, politician, postmaster, and author? Benjamin Franklin was born in Boston, Massachusetts on January 17, 1706. He lived for 84 years. Franklin was one of our country's "Founding Fathers". He signed the Declaration of Independence, the Treaty of Paris and the U.S. Constitution. He is well known for his experiment with electricity, the kite and key with lightning during a thunderstorm. Franklin invented glasses called bifocals, too. Some of your grandparents may even have or remember his invention called the Franklin stove. One of his famous writings is Poor Richard's Almanac. It was written years ago and is still published and bought today. In this book, he gives facts about weather, and recipes. He wrote funny sayings and jokes in his works, too.

5. What did you learn from reading this story? Mark those that apply.

Ⓐ Benjamin Franklin was a Founding Father of our country.
Ⓑ Benjamin Franklin was an author and wrote Poor Richard's Almanac.
Ⓒ Benjamin Franklin was a skinny man with glasses.
Ⓓ He invented bifocals and the Franklin stove.

6. Fill in the words below to complete the sentences about Mr. Franklin.

U.S. Constitution
84
Founding Fathers
electricity

a. Franklin did experiments with a key, and kite during a thunderstorm to show _____.

b. Benjamin Franklin is one of our country's _____.

c. He lived to be _____ years old.

d. Mr. Franklin signed the Declaration of Independence, the Treaty of Paris and the _____.

7. List the 6 jobs that Mr. Franklin held as stated in the story.

8. What do you think the purpose of this text is? Write your own sentence

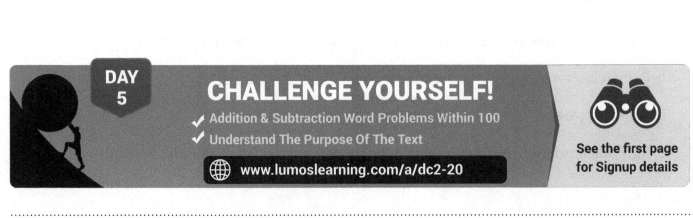

DAY 5

CHALLENGE YOURSELF!
✔ Addition & Subtraction Word Problems Within 100
✔ Understand The Purpose Of The Text

🌐 www.lumoslearning.com/a/dc2-20

See the first page
for Signup details

SWIMMING
7 TIPS TO BECOME A BETTER SWIMMER

Just about everyone knows how to swim, or at least play around in the water. But you want to be a competitive swimmer, so how do you set yourself apart from all those people who just want to hang out at the pool? Here's a guide on how to take it to the next level.

1. Make Time for Practice

The best swimmers spend the most amount of time in the pool practicing their technique. While natural ability gives some people an advantage, the great ones are the ones who keep practicing.

Set aside time each day for some sort of swimming activity or exercise that you can do. Even if you don't have access to a pool every day, there's tons of exercises and drills that you can do to build strength and endurance. Make a plan and stick to it.

2. Know Your Sport

Freestyle swimming is the most common and well-known forms of swimming. A stroke is the full circle motion your arm makes when swimming. A freestyle stroke can be broken down into four phases. Those phases are catch, pull, exit, and recovery.

The catch phase is when your hand goes out in front of you and hits the water. In the pull phase, your hand goes underwater and down toward the bottom of the pool. In this phase, you are "pulling" yourself through the water. The exit phase is when your hand is coming up from the bottom of the pull phase. Your hand comes up from the bottom and comes up beside your leg. In the recovery phase, your arm is out of the water and rotates back towards the catch.

3. Improve Each Phase of the Stroke

Try swimming with your hand closed during the catch and pull phases. This will increase your forearm strength and help improve your stroke.

During the exit phase, flick your wrist at the end before it comes out of the water.

During the recovery phase, focus on getting your hand and arm back in the water as quickly as possible. The longer your hand is out of the water, the less time you spend pulling yourself forward.

4. Build Your Strength

To improve your swimming ability, you will need to improve your strength. Body weight exercises can be done anywhere and aren't likely to cause injury like weight lifting can.

Exercises like push-ups and pull-ups strengthen your upper body. Doing these exercises will help you when you are pulling through the water.

Lunges, squats, and calf raises strengthen your lower body. These exercises will help you when you are kicking your legs, giving you more speed through the water.

Core exercises focus on your stomach, sides, lower back, and hips. Exercises such as crunches, leg raises, and bicycle kicks give your core a great workout. Strengthening your core will help you keep great form throughout your swim.

5. Increase Your Endurance

Even when you aren't in the pool, you can keep active to improve your endurance. Endurance exercises like biking and running help build your lung capacity so you can swim longer. Sprinting will help build muscle endurance so you can swim faster and harder without getting tired.

6. Breathing

It is important to learn to breathe correctly when swimming. New swimmers have a habit of bringing their head out of the water and breathing through their mouth.

Instead of bringing your head all the way out of the water, take breaths through your nose as you turn your head to the side. Practice this technique in shallow water without swimming, then try it while swimming.

7. Find a Good Coach.

Even the most successful athletes have coaches. A good coach can set you up with an exercise program. The coach also gets to see you swim on a regular basis. That way she can tell you what you might be doing wrong and help correct it.

And most importantly, remember to have fun!

WEEK 5
SUMMER PRACTICE

REPRESENT WHOLE NUMBERS AS LENGTHS ON A NUMBER LINE

1. 54 + ___ = 74

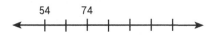

- Ⓐ 10
- Ⓑ 4
- Ⓒ 64
- Ⓓ 20

2. If you start at 15 and jump three times, what number will you land on?

- Ⓐ 30
- Ⓑ 25
- Ⓒ 15
- Ⓓ 5

3. How many times will you jump to show 22 + 6?

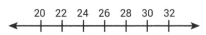

- Ⓐ 2
- Ⓑ 3
- Ⓒ 6
- Ⓓ 8

4. How many times will you jump to get from 35 to 45?

- Ⓐ 1
- Ⓑ 10
- Ⓒ 2
- Ⓓ 5

Read the text below. Reread it at least three times to help you. The words in bold may be new words for you. To use context clues in a text, it is important to read all the sentences around the new word. This will help you understand the meaning of the new words. After you have read the text many times, use what you learn to answer the questions about the new vocabulary.

Regional temperatures are changing with the climate. This change in certain areas of the country makes it hard for plants and animals to live. Animals may need to relocate to places that have the temperatures they are used to living in. This move can be difficult for them. This change may cause some **species** to move farther north where the weather is cooler or farther south where the weather is warmer. Many kinds of animals migrate each year and more are doing so with the climate changes. With the changes in climate, there may be different places in which plants can still grow in certain areas. The land and water are also affected. Researchers use data to help them understand these changes. Reports, charts, graphs, and daily monitoring of land is detailed in the information gathered. Currents in the oceans have impact on the climate changes, too. The speed and direction of the water moving on the ocean floor is being studied to help add more information. Scientists hope this research will help them understand more about climate change.

5. Which is the best definition of the word "Regional"?

Ⓐ   Cities in the country
Ⓑ   Certain areas of the country
Ⓒ   A way to get data for the scientists
Ⓓ   Climate change

6. Why do animals relocate? Write a sentence that explains.

7. Highlight the set of under lined words that help you in understanding the word "species".

This change may cause some species to move farther north where the weather is cooler or farther south where the weather is warmer. Many kinds of animals migrate each year and more are doing so with the climate changes.

8. List what scientists use in their "data".

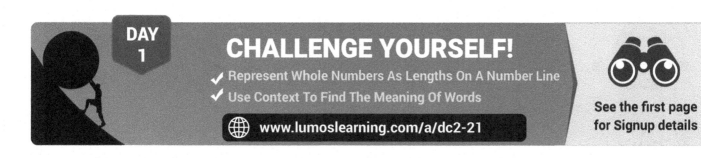

DAY 1

CHALLENGE YOURSELF!

✔ Represent Whole Numbers As Lengths On A Number Line
✔ Use Context To Find The Meaning Of Words

🌐 www.lumoslearning.com/a/dc2-21

See the first page
for Signup details

1. What time is shown on the clock below?

- Ⓐ 5:05
- Ⓑ 6:01
- Ⓒ 1:06
- Ⓓ 6:05

2. What time is shown on the clock below?

- Ⓐ 11:15
- Ⓑ 3:55
- Ⓒ 11:03
- Ⓓ 11:20

3. What time is shown on the clock below?

- Ⓐ 9:30
- Ⓑ 8:06
- Ⓒ 8:30
- Ⓓ 8:15

4. Mark has basketball practice at the time that is shown on the clock. What time does Mark have basketball practice.

- Ⓐ 4:45
- Ⓑ 4:00
- Ⓒ 3:45
- Ⓓ 3:09

5. Collective nouns show a group of things. Read the sentences below and choose the collective noun in each sentence. Highlight the collective noun.

We saw a flock of geese in the sky.
Mama said that our cat had a litter of kittens.
Buzzing around us was a swarm of bees.
The pack of wolves howled in the night.

6. Read the list of collective nouns and choose the right one for each group to describe it.

flock
bunch
swarm
herd

Group	Collective Noun
Cows	
Bananas	
Birds	
Flies	

7. Mark the sentences that have collective nouns in them.

Ⓐ We looked for the deck of cards.
Ⓑ Sara picked up the wash.
Ⓒ The children were playing on the playground.
Ⓓ There was a colony of ants in our garden.

8. Which of the following phrases does NOT have a collective noun in it? Mark your answer.

Ⓐ ran to the store
Ⓑ band of soldiers
Ⓒ bundle of papers
Ⓓ bunch of grapes

DAY
2

CHALLENGE YOURSELF!
✔ Tell And Write Time From Clocks
✔ People, Places, and Things

 www.lumoslearning.com/a/dc2-22

See the first page
for Signup details

1. How much money in all is 1 dollar, 3 dimes, and 4 pennies?

Ⓐ $1.19
Ⓑ $1.79
Ⓒ $1.30
Ⓓ $1.34

2. What is the value of 2 quarters, 3 dimes, 4 nickels, and 1 penny?

Ⓐ $1.01
Ⓑ $2.01
Ⓒ $0.91
Ⓓ $1.41

3. What is the value of 3 dollars, 4 quarters, and 6 pennies?

Ⓐ $4.46
Ⓑ $3.46
Ⓒ $4.06
Ⓓ $3.64

4. Billy has 6 quarters, 3 dimes, and 2 nickels. How much money does Billy have in all?

Ⓐ $1.80
Ⓑ $1.90
Ⓒ $2.80
Ⓓ $2.90

5. Read the words below and mark the right boxes.

	Noun	Adjective	Verb	Adverb
little				
elephant				
really				
walking				
quickly				
running				
fuzzy				
slipper				

6. Read each group of words below. A complete sentence must have a subject and predicate. The subject has the noun in it. The predicate has the verb in it. Mark the 2 sentences that are complete and make sense.

Ⓐ Fishing near the lake.
Ⓑ Margie and I love to go hiking in the woods.
Ⓒ Tracy is happy that he has a new little baby brother.
Ⓓ Skipping down the sidewalk while it is raining.

7. Read the phrase below. Decide what part of the sentence is missing. Write your answers in the blank. The sentence is missing a subject or predicate.

ran a long way home	
My friends and I	
Grandma and Grandpa	
skipping in the rain	

8. Write the right verb for each sentence below. Be careful, each word can only be used one time. (ran, follow, bake, see, draw)

a. We like to .... pictures in Art Class.

b. She would not .... the directions the teacher told us.

c. I .... all the way home when I was late for dinner.

d. Grandma will .... my favorite birthday cake!

e. Did you .... her look of surprise?

DAY 3

CHALLENGE YOURSELF!
✔ Solve Word Problems Involving Money
✔ Language Conventions

🌐 www.lumoslearning.com/a/dc2-23

See the first page for Signup details

The measurement of Kim's pieces of ribbon are plotted on the line plot. Use the line plot below to answer all the questions.

Note: Each x represents 2 pieces of ribbon

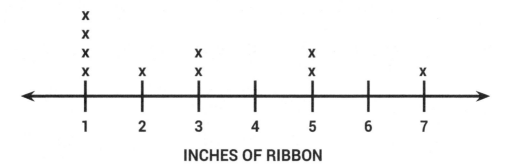

INCHES OF RIBBON

1. What lengths does none of Kim's ribbons measure?

Ⓐ   1 inch and 2 inches
Ⓑ   4 inches and 5 inches
Ⓒ   4 inches and 6 inches
Ⓓ   2 inches and 7 inches

2. How many pieces of ribbon does Kim have that is 7 inches?

Ⓐ   2
Ⓑ   1
Ⓒ   3
Ⓓ   0

3. How many pieces of Kim's ribbon is only 1 inch long?

Ⓐ   4
Ⓑ   2
Ⓒ   8
Ⓓ   6

4. Kim can only use the ribbon that is 3 or more inches. How many pieces of ribbon can Kim use?

Ⓐ   5
Ⓑ   10
Ⓒ   4
Ⓓ   12

5. When there is more of one thing, some words need an "s" added to them.

Examples: tree becomes trees, plane becomes planes.
Singular means one and plural means more than one.

Some words must be changed to become plural.
If a noun ends in "lf", you change the "f" to a "v" and add "es".
Change the words from singular to plural.

wolf	
shelf	
leaf	
knife	
elf	

6. To make words ending in a "y" to plural, you change the "y" to "I" and add "es".
   Read the list of words below and make them plural.

butterfly	
fly	
story	
baby	

7. To make some words plural you add "es". Make the singular words match the plurals in the table below.

potato	
tomato	
wish	
bench	
box	

8. Sometimes when a noun becomes plural, the word changes all together. Read the sentences below. The underlined word is singular and should be plural. Mark the correct plural noun.

a. She was afraid of mouse.

Ⓐ mouses
Ⓑ mice

b. All the person were happy!

Ⓐ people
Ⓑ peoples

c. I heard so many goose honking at the park.

Ⓐ geeses
Ⓑ geese

d. Her foot had grown, and her shoes did not fit.

Ⓐ foots
Ⓑ feet

DAY 4

CHALLENGE YOURSELF!

✔ Generate Measurement Data
✔ Regular and Irregular Plural Nouns

 www.lumoslearning.com/a/dc2-24

See the first page for Signup details

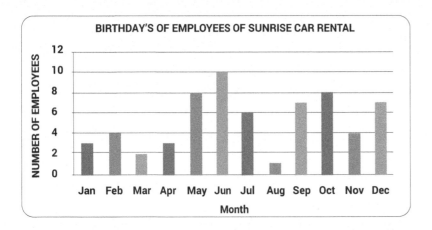

Use the bar graph to answer following questions.

1. Which month had the fewest number of employee birthdays?

Ⓐ August
Ⓑ June
Ⓒ March
Ⓓ January

2. How many employees have a birthday in January?

Ⓐ 2
Ⓑ 4
Ⓒ 2 ½
Ⓓ 3

3. Which month had the most employee birthdays?

Ⓐ May
Ⓑ June
Ⓒ August
Ⓓ March

4. If Sunrise Car Rental gets a new employee that has a birthday in December, how many employees will have December birthdays?

Ⓐ 7
Ⓑ 8
Ⓒ 9
Ⓓ 6

Reflexive pronouns tell about the subject.
Example: herself, myself, ourselves, himself, themselves, yourself.

5. Read the sentences and highlight the reflexive pronoun in each sentence.

The children helped themselves to bake.

I see myself as a ballerina.

Maggy knows how to sew by herself.

We tell ourselves to be nice to each other

6. Read the sentences and decide what is the subject and what is the reflexive pronoun in each one.

1. I did it myself.
2. She made herself a cake.
3. We ran by ourselves to the park.

Subject	Reflexive pronoun

7. Choose the right reflexive pronoun for each sentence. Write it in the blank.

a. We understood the directions by _____.
   (themselves, ourselves)

b. She watched the baby by _____.
   (herself, himself)

c. They cannot do it _____.
   (ourselves, themselves)

d. He made the kite _____.
   (herself, himself)

8. Which of the following sentences does NOT have a reflexive pronoun in it?

Ⓐ Mark ran the mile by himself.
Ⓑ Sarah and Tammy played the piano.
Ⓒ Tyrone caught himself a huge fish.
Ⓓ They made pies themselves.

LumosLearning.com

MAZE GAME

Help Santa Claus find the Christmas tree

MAZE GAME

Help fox find mushroom

MAZE GAME

Help rabbit find carrot

MAZE GAME

Help squirrel find acorn

WEEK 6
SUMMER PRACTICE

RECOGNIZE AND DRAW SHAPES

1. Which shape is shown below?

![rectangle shape]

Ⓐ Square
Ⓑ Rhombus
Ⓒ Rectangle
Ⓓ Triangle

2. Which shape has four equal sides?

Ⓐ Rectangle
Ⓑ Square
Ⓒ Hexagon
Ⓓ Triangle

3. Which shape is the face of a cube?

Ⓐ Triangle
Ⓑ Square
Ⓒ Rectangle
Ⓓ Circle

4. Which shape is shown below?

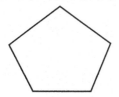

Ⓐ Triangle
Ⓑ Hexagon
Ⓒ Pentagon
Ⓓ Octagon

Read the text below and answer the question that follows.

Verbs tell the action in a sentence. They are a part of the predicate. Some verbs can be changed from what is happening now (present tense) to what happened before (past tense). Most verbs are changed from present to past by adding an "ed". But some do not follow that rule. An irregular past tense verb is one where either the verb is changed to a new word or stays the same in present and past tense.

5. **What do verbs do in a sentence? Mark the two best answers.**

Ⓐ Verbs name the noun in the sentence.
Ⓑ Verbs tell the action in a sentence.
Ⓒ Verbs are words in a sentence that tell about the subject.
Ⓓ Verbs are part of the predicate.

6. **Fill in the blank to answer the sentence about irregular verbs. Use what you read to help you.**

An irregular past tense verb is one where either ....

....

7. **Below is a list of present and past tense verbs. Mark the irregular verbs that tell what has already happened (past tense).**

Ⓐ sat
Ⓑ hide
Ⓒ tell
Ⓓ ate
Ⓔ sit
Ⓕ hid
Ⓖ told
Ⓗ eat

8. Read the sentences and pick the correct irregular past tense verb to answer each one.

a. Yesterday we _____ to the bus.

   (run, ran)

b. Last Saturday, Mary _____ shopping with her mother.

   (went, go)

c. They _____ the deer when they went on vacation a month ago.

   (saw, see)

d. When I was in first grade, Mr. Samuel _____ me how to read.

   (teach, taught)

LumosLearning.com

DAY
2

1. Which shape is portioned into 3 rows and 4 columns?

Ⓐ

Ⓑ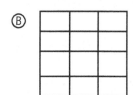

Ⓒ

Ⓓ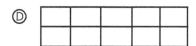

2. Which shape is portioned into 4 columns and 5 rows?

Ⓐ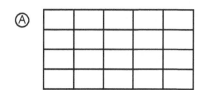

Ⓑ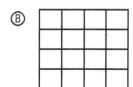

Ⓒ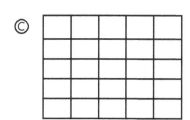

Ⓓ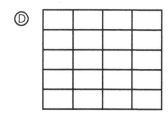

3. How many rows and columns are in the shape below?

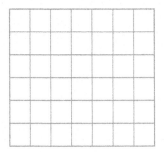

Ⓐ   5 rows, 5 columns
Ⓑ   4 rows, 5 columns
Ⓒ   6 rows, 6 columns
Ⓓ   4 columns, 5 rows

4. How many rows and columns are in the shape below?

Ⓐ   6 rows, 6 columns
Ⓑ   7 rows, 6 columns
Ⓒ   6 rows, 7 columns
Ⓓ   7 rows, 7 columns

Sentences must have a subject (noun and any describing words) and predicate (verb and any helping words) to be complete. If words put together do not have both a subject and a verb they do not make a sentence. These words are phrases.

5. Part A
Let's look at the story below. Some of the words are not in a complete sentence. Highlight the words (phrases) that are not a complete sentence.

Mary and Jane want. to go to the store. They got ready. Mary asked her mother. for some money. Her mother gave her $2. Jane got $5 from her dad.

Part B
Make the phrases that were not complete sentences, complete by putting them together. Be sure to take out the period and join the words. Write them below.

6. Write the three complete sentences from the story. Reread the story.

Mary and Jane want. to go to the store. They got ready. Mary asked her mother. for some money. Her mother gave her $2. Jane got $5 from her dad.

7. Read the phrases below. Fill the subject to the boxes to make the sentence complete.

Roberto and Miguel
The beautiful ponies
She
The chicken soup

Subject	Predicate
	were fun to ride.
	love to play football.
	was good to eat.
	brushed her hair.

8. Read the predicates and match them with the correct subjects. Use each one only one time to make the best sentences.

Betty
The race car
The dish
The alarm

Subject	Predicate
	sped down the hill.
	broke as it fell to the floor.
	started ringing when the fire
	began.
	rode her bike up the road.

DAY 2

CHALLENGE YOURSELF!
✔ Partition a Rectangle Into Rows And Columns
✔ Simple And Compound Sentences

🌐 www.lumoslearning.com/a/dc2-27

See the first page for Signup details

1. Which shape is portioned into two halves?

Ⓐ

Ⓑ

Ⓒ

2. Which shape is portioned into thirds?

Ⓐ

Ⓑ

Ⓒ

3. Which shape is portioned into fourths?

Ⓐ

Ⓑ

Ⓒ

4. What choice best describes the shaded part below?

Ⓐ One-Third
Ⓑ One-Fourth
Ⓒ One-Half

5. Highlight the proper nouns in the sentences below.

The little puppy made Sarah very happy.
They went to see the show in Dallas Texas
If you love candy,you will love Valentine's Day!
John and Skipper played ball on Saturday.

6. The names of products are capitalized, too. An example is Cheetos. It names the snack. If you had the word chips, it would not be capitalized. It did not tell the product name of chips. Read the list in the box. Mark the ones that name or do not name a particular product.

	Names a particular product	Does not name a particular product
Cheerios cereal		
popcorn		
Skippy peanut butter		
Kraft cheese		

7. We know that a comma is used in a list of words, and to join clauses in sentences. Commas are also used in the headings and closings of letters. For example- Dear Mom, is an example of how to use a comma when you start a letter. For the closing of a letter here is an example- Yours truly, - then your name would go on the next line.

Read the list and Mark the ones that use a comma correctly.

Ⓐ Dear Mayor,
Ⓑ Thank, you
Ⓒ Dearest Grandma,
Ⓓ Respectfully,

8. The apostrophe mark ' is used to combine two words into one word to make a contraction. If the word "not" is the second word in the sentence, take out the letter "o", put in the ' and make the contraction. Read the list of words and make them into contractions. Write the new word.

a. should not = _____

b. is not =_____

c. did not =_____

DAY 3

CHALLENGE YOURSELF!

✔ Partition Circles And Rectangles
✔ Understand Language Conventions

 www.lumoslearning.com/a/dc2-28

See the first page for Signup details

1. Jimmy exercised for 36 minutes on Monday. He exercised for 12 more minutes on Tuesday, than he did on Monday. How many minutes did Jimmy exercise in all for both Monday and Tuesday?

   Ⓐ 48
   Ⓑ 24
   Ⓒ 38
   Ⓓ 84

2. Mark earned a 98 on his Math quiz this week. He earned 11 points higher this week than he earned on his quiz last week. What grade did Mark earn on last week's quiz?

3. Put a check mark under the correct equation to solve each word problem.

	34+17=?	34−17=?
Lisa had 34 books. She read 17. How many books did she not read?		
Lisa bought 17 books. She had 34. How many books does Lisa have now?		

4. Brittney and Joshua are saving their money to buy a new video game for $59. Brittney has $26 saved and Joshua has $19 saved. Answer below questions.

How much money have Brittney and Joshua saved altogether?	
How much more money does Brittney have saved than Joshua?	
How much more money do they need to save to buy the video game?	

5. Remember that holidays are always capitalized. Read the list of words and mark the holidays.

- Ⓐ Easter
- Ⓑ Eggs
- Ⓒ Memorial Day
- Ⓓ Valentine's Day
- Ⓔ Presents

6. Read the sentences below. Mark the one that uses capitalization correctly for holidays.

- Ⓐ The family went on a vacation for the fourth of July
- Ⓑ Mary and her mother made cupcakes for Veteran's Day.
- Ⓒ The team rode in a parade on president's day.
- Ⓓ Grandpa does not like halloween.

7. Names of products are capitalized, too. Examples of these are Cheerios for a cereal, and Kraft for cheese or milk products. If an exact name is not there, do not capitalize it. Read the words in the box and mark if they should be capitalized.

	Capitalize	Do not capitalize
Ford		
Truck		
Amazon		
Dog food		
M & M's		
Candy		
Store		
Coca Cola		

8. Read the sentences below. Mark the two that use product names correctly.

- Ⓐ Most people like to eat Lay's chips.
- Ⓑ He drove a bright shiny Toyota truck.
- Ⓒ The dentist says to use crest toothpaste.
- Ⓓ We feed our dog purina dog chow.

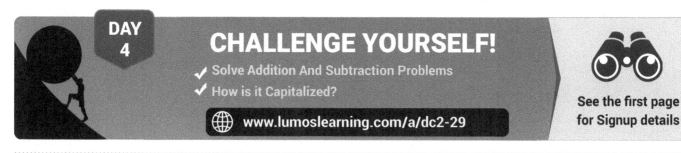

DAY 4

CHALLENGE YOURSELF!
✔ Solve Addition And Subtraction Problems
✔ How is it Capitalized?

🌐 www.lumoslearning.com/a/dc2-29

See the first page for Signup details

1. Select all of the equations that have a difference of 4.

Ⓐ 17 - 4 = ?
Ⓑ 12 - 8 = ?
Ⓒ 19 - 15 = ?
Ⓓ 20 - 5 = ?
Ⓔ 10 - 6 = ?

2. What number added to itself equals 14?

3. Place a check mark under the correct column to tell whether the equation equals 12 or does not equal 12.

	Equals 12	Does not Equal 12
14 + 3=?		
11 + 1=?		
20 - 8=?		
18 - 6=?		
2 + 10=?		

4. Complete the table by filling in the missing number in each equation.

15	+		=	17
19	-	7	=	
	+	5	=	7
18	-		=	3

5. Commas are used in greetings of letters and closings.
Choose the answers that are correct use of a comma in the greeting of a letter.

Ⓐ Dear Calvin,
Ⓑ Dearest Aunt Sue
Ⓒ Dearest Grandmother
Ⓓ To Whom It May Concern,
Ⓔ Dear William

6. Read the letter. In both the start of a letter (salutation) and end of a letter (closing), a comma should be used at the end. Check and make the corrections if needed by adding a comma.

Dear Daddy

I would like to thank you for the gift of a new bike. It is the best gift ever. I love the basket on the front and the bright red color of the seat.

Thanks again
L' Toya

7. Mark the correct answer that shows how to use a comma at the beginning of the letter.

Ⓐ Dear David
Ⓑ Dear Tabitha
Ⓒ Dear Franklin
Ⓓ Dear Aunt Bea,

8. Read the following salutations. Fix the ones that are not correct by rewriting them with a comma.

To the President   Dear Eddie   Dear Mom,   Hello Friend,

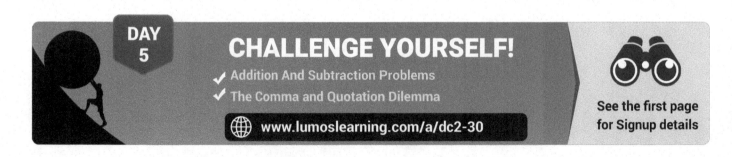

LumosLearning.com

WEEK 7
SUMMER PRACTICE

GROUPS OF ODD AND EVEN NUMBERS

1. Select all of the numbers that are even.

- Ⓐ 61
- Ⓑ 89
- Ⓒ 98
- Ⓓ 16
- Ⓔ 24

2. Choose all of the equations that will equal an odd number.

- Ⓐ 5+6=?
- Ⓑ 3+7=?
- Ⓒ 8+10=?
- Ⓓ 4+3=?
- Ⓔ 9+2=?

3. In her drawer, Carrie has 9 pairs of socks and 1 sock she could not find a match for. How many socks does Carrie have in her drawer?

4. Choose if each group of circle represents an even or odd number.

	EVEN	ODD
OOOOOOO OOOOOO		
OOOOOOOO OOOOOOOO		
OOOO + OOO = ?		
OO + OOOO = ?		

5. Contractions are made by joining two words into one word and leaving out a letter. You put an ' in place of the missing letter to make the contraction. Some kinds of contractions combine a word with the word "are". The letter "a" is then left out and the 'put in. Some kinds combine a word with the word "is". The letter "i" is left out and the ' put in. Read the first word and second word in each row and write contractions in the contraction column.

First word	Second word	Contraction
they	are	
we	are	
she	is	
he	is	
you	are	

6. Which two sentences have contractions in them? Mark them.

Ⓐ   Jamie and I played in the park with our friends.
Ⓑ   We aren't going to go shopping until Friday.
Ⓒ   They're happy to go on vacation.
Ⓓ   She ran home for supper.

7. Write the contractions with the words below using not as the second word. Remember to leave out the "o" in not and add an '.

a. are = _____

b. have = _____

c. did = _____

d. is = _____

8. There are a couple of words that change completely when not is added as the second word and a contraction is made. Will not becomes won't and cannot becomes can't. Pick the sentence below that has one of these contractions in it. Mark your answer.

Ⓐ   Latifa can go into town with us.
Ⓑ   The cows will eat their hay when it gets cold.
Ⓒ   The firemen won't let the fire spread.
Ⓓ   The police helped the lady cross the street.

DAY 1

CHALLENGE YOURSELF!
✔ Groups Of Odd And Even Numbers
✔ Use An Apostrophe

🌐 www.lumoslearning.com/a/dc2-31

See the first page
for Signup details

1. Select TWO equations that are represented by the array.

- Ⓐ 5+5+5=?
- Ⓑ 3×5=?
- Ⓒ 3+3+3?
- Ⓓ 3×3=?

2. Select TWO equations that are represented by the array.

- Ⓐ 5×2=?
- Ⓑ 5+5+5+5+5=?
- Ⓒ 2×2=?
- Ⓓ 2+2+2+2+2=?

3. At band practice, there are 5 rows and 4 students in each row. How many students are at band practice?

4. Match each array to one of the sums by placing a check mark under the correct column.

	12	18
OOO OOO OOO OOO		
OOOOOOOOO OOOOOOOOO		
OOOO OOOO OOOO		
OOOOOO OOOOOO OOOOOO		

5. **Spelling has patterns in words that help us to remember how to spell them. Here is a pattern for spelling.**
   If a word has a short vowel sound and ends in the "k" sound, the "k" sound is spelled"ck".
   Read the words below and mark the ones that follow this rule.

   Ⓐ Bike
   Ⓑ Back
   Ⓒ Rack
   Ⓓ Stick
   Ⓔ Flick
   Ⓕ Brake
   Ⓖ Like
   Ⓗ Lake

6. **If a word ends in the long "a" sound, the spelling pattern at the end is "ay". Choose YES or NO for each word in the box to show if the word follows this rule.**

	Yes	No
play		
stay		
away		
bake		
story		

7. **A spelling pattern for long e words is that the long "e" is usually spelled with "ee" or "ea" and sometimes "ie" when followed by the letter "c". Long e can also be spelled e in short words such as me, he, she be, and we. The word "the" is not usually long "e", but the "e" says "u" like in duck.**

   Read the sentences below and Mark the long "e" spelled words. (Do not mark the word "the".)
   There can be more than one long "e" word in each sentence.

   We looked for the cat that ran up the tree.
   Sandra and I would like to eat a piece of chocolate cake.
   Please wash your hands.
   The ice will freeze in about an hour.

8. Read the words. Mark the ones that have the long "e" spelling.

Ⓐ Better
Ⓑ Beef
Ⓒ Step
Ⓓ Sleep
Ⓔ Meat
Ⓕ Met

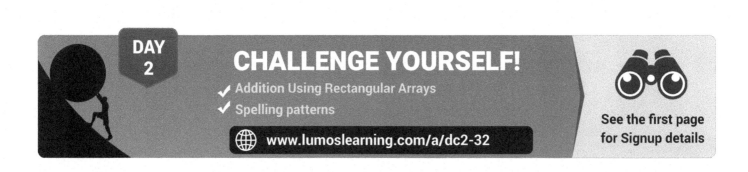

DAY 2

CHALLENGE YOURSELF!
✔ Addition Using Rectangular Arrays
✔ Spelling patterns

🌐 www.lumoslearning.com/a/dc2-32

See the first page for Signup details

1. Choose a number that does not have any hundreds.

Ⓐ 300
Ⓑ 58
Ⓒ 700
Ⓓ 900

2. Choose a number that does not have any ones.

Ⓐ 809
Ⓑ 340
Ⓒ 209
Ⓓ 33

3. How many tens are bundled to make one hundred?

4. Place a check mark under each column of the correct number.

	583	385	853	538
8 ones, 3 tens, 5 hundreds				
8 hundreds, 5 tens, 3 ones				
8 tens, 3 ones, 5 hundreds				
5 ones, 3 hundreds, 8 tens				

5. Dictionaries help you to spell, pronounce, and understand what words mean. The two guide words at the top of the pages show you if the word you want is on that page. The words on the page fall between the words in ABC order.

If I wanted to check the spelling of the word - giraffe - which guide words would I use in a dictionary? Mark the best answer.

Ⓐ dairy - doghouse
Ⓑ germ - great
Ⓒ gem - get
Ⓓ fairy - fun

6. Read the sentence below. Then read the definitions for the words from a dictionary. Which word fits best in the sentence? Mark the answer.
He was _____ to see his friends.

Ⓐ Explosive - might become violent, dangerous
Ⓑ Excited - eager, enthusiastic, anticipating emotions
Ⓒ Skinny - narrow, slender, thin

7. Which two words need to be looked up in the dictionary to correct the spelling?

Ⓐ happy
Ⓑ forgeting
Ⓒ childran
Ⓓ complete

8. An online encyclopedia gives information about a topic. It can be used to help you write a report or understand more about something. Which 3 topics would you find the most information about in an online encyclopedia? Mark the ones that would help you research topics.

Ⓐ Funny
Ⓑ Rainforest
Ⓒ Trees
Ⓓ Walking
Ⓔ Cats

DAY 3

CHALLENGE YOURSELF!
✓ Three Digit Numbers
✓ Consult Reference Materials

 www.lumoslearning.com/a/dc2-33

See the first page
for Signup details

1. 80 tens equals how many hundreds?

Ⓐ 80
Ⓑ 8
Ⓒ 800
Ⓓ 88

2. How many groups of hundred can be made from the blocks below?

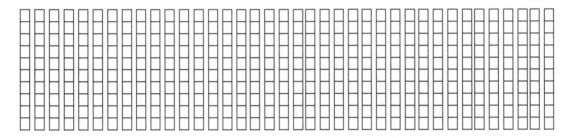

Ⓐ 300
Ⓑ 30
Ⓒ 3
Ⓓ 380

3. Josh drew 6 hundred base-blocks and 10 ten base-blocks. How many hundreds did Josh's drawing represent?

4. Blake said that 700 ones is more than 70 tens. Is he correct? Explain your answer.

Read the story and answer the questions.

It was a nice sunny day outside. Noe and Kevin wanted to ride their bikes to the park. The boys were at Noe's house. They had ridden bikes the day before. Kevin had spent the night with Noe. When they got ready, they noticed their tires were low on air and they needed to fix them.

The boys looked in the garage. Luckily, they found a tire pump. In no time, they had their bikes ready to go!

5. Where were the boys? Mark the answer.

Ⓐ   At the park
Ⓑ   At Noe's grandma's house
Ⓒ   At Kevin's house
Ⓓ   At Noe's house

6. Who are the characters in the story? Write them.

7. What was the problem in the story? Write your own answer.

8. **If you were to give a speech about making a sandwich which two sentences below would be the best ideas to use?**

Ⓐ You could get the materials and make the sandwich while you were talking about it.
Ⓑ You could pass out notes to the class, so they could follow along.
Ⓒ You could eat the sandwich.
Ⓓ You could ask your little brother for help.

DAY 4

CHALLENGE YOURSELF!
✔ Count In Hundreds
✔ Use Knowledge Of Language And Its Conventions

🌐 www.lumoslearning.com/a/dc2-34

See the first page for Signup details

1. Start at 210 and count by 5's. What is the 6th number you say?

Ⓐ 710
Ⓑ 270
Ⓒ 770
Ⓓ 240

2. Identify the pattern of the numbers by placing a check-mark under the column.

	5s	10s	100s
310, 410, 510, 610, 710, 810			
305, 310, 315, 320, 325, 330			
715, 725, 735, 745, 755, 765			
400, 405, 410, 415, 420, 425			

3. Complete the table by filling in the missing numbers from each pattern.

	545	555		575
803				843
	325	425		
800			830	

4. Ted says that you can start at any number and count by 10s and every number in the pattern will end in a zero. Is Ted correct? Explain your answer.

We speak in different ways when we talk to different people.

Informal speaking is a way we talk to friends and relatives. Formal speaking is a way we talk to people we do not know very well.

5. Read the names in the box and mark if we would talk to them informal or formal.

Word	Informal	Formal
Mother		
Classmate		
Best friend		
Mayor		
President		
Grandma		

6. Read the sentences and write formal or informal after each one.

a. "Hey, let's go swimming!"

b. "Your Honor, would like to invite you to attend our banquet."

c. "This is to inform you of your required attendance."

d. "Let's get this party going!"

e. "Mr. President, we are proud of you.

7. Which 2 sentences are informal?

Ⓐ "Mom, I am hungry!"
Ⓑ "Enter the building through the door."
Ⓒ "Pay your bill on time."
Ⓓ "Yeah, we won the game!"

8. Your teacher told the class to write a letter to the City Council. Which type of English would you use? Formal or Informal?

DAY 5

CHALLENGE YOURSELF!

✔ Count Within 1000
✔ Formal and Informal Language

 www.lumoslearning.com/a/dc2-35

See the first page for Signup details

CROSS WORD PUZZLES

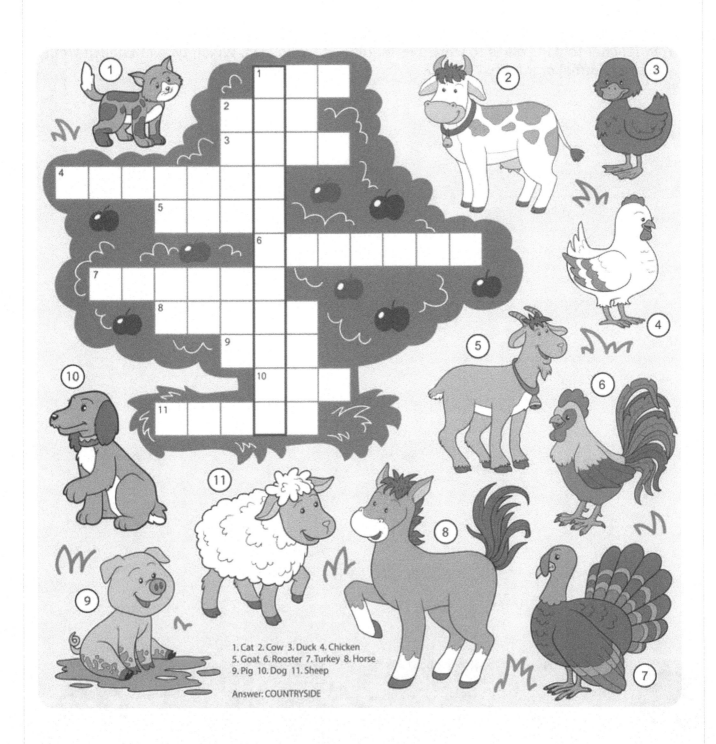

1. Cat 2. Cow 3. Duck 4. Chicken
5. Goat 6. Rooster 7. Turkey 8. Horse
9. Pig 10. Dog 11. Sheep

Answer: COUNTRYSIDE

WEEK 8
SUMMER PRACTICE

DAY 1

1. Choose the comparison that is correct.

Ⓐ   400 + 50 + 2 < 400 + 20 + 5
Ⓑ   312 > 300 + 20 + 1
Ⓒ   400 + 60 + 2 = 462
Ⓓ   900 = 900 + 90

2. Select all of the comparisons that are correct.

Ⓐ   413 < 400 + 30 + 1
Ⓑ   500 + 60 + 8 = 568
Ⓒ   100 + 70 + 7 > 700 + 70 + 1
Ⓓ   200 + 2 < 200 + 20
Ⓔ   777 = 700 + 70

3. Which number is the greatest between 324, 342, 234, 243?

4. Place a check mark under the correct column to complete each comparison.

	>	<	=
459 ___ 495			
233 ___ 200 + 30 + 1			
700 + 70 ___ 700 + 7			
200 + 40 ___ 240			

Prefixes are letters added to words to form new words with different meanings. Read the prefix and what it means.

5. Write the definitions of each new word that is made when the prefix is added.
   For example - unlocked - not locked.
                    un - not

   a. unhappy - _____

   b. unopened - _____

   c. unable - _____

   d. unknown - _____

6. Read the sentences below. Mark the sentence that has a prefix word in it that means "not".

   Ⓐ He isn't going to the fair because he is sick.
   Ⓑ She untied her shoelaces.
   Ⓒ He is looking for the answer to the question.
   Ⓓ She will reread the book to better understand it.

7. Read the prefix and what it means.
   Write the definitions of each new word that is made when the prefix is added.
   Example: remake – make again re – again, back

   a. reread - _____

   b. replay - _____

   c. redo - _____

8. The prefix "pre" means before. Read the sentences and highlight the words that have this prefix in it.

Her little sister went to preschool in the city.

Mom had to preheat the oven before she could cook her supper.

DAY
1
CHALLENGE YOURSELF!
✔ Compare Two Three-digit Numbers
✔ Prefix and Suffix

🌐 www.lumoslearning.com/a/dc2-36

See the first page
for Signup details

1. Select all of the equations that equal 68.

- Ⓐ 78 − 10 = ?
- Ⓑ 34 + 34 = ?
- Ⓒ 100 − 28 = ?
- Ⓓ 22 + 46 = ?
- Ⓔ 58 + 20 = ?

2. Select all of the equations that equal 23.

- Ⓐ 53 − 33 = ?
- Ⓑ 19 + 5 = ?
- Ⓒ 65 − 42 = ?
- Ⓓ 3 + 20 = ?
- Ⓔ 11 + 23 = ?

3. What number does x represent in the equation?
   54 + x = 75

4. Match each equation with the number it equals by placing a check-mark under the correct column.

	27	18	32
23 + ? = 41			
62 - ? = 30			
48 - ? = 21			

Adjectives and adverbs are words used in sentences. Adjectives tell about nouns while adverbs tell about verbs, adjectives or another adverb.

5. Read the list of noun phrases. Write the adjectives.

noun phrases	adjectives
purple flowers	
second-grade teacher	
yellow bright light	
funny smile	
grumpy old man	
good grades	

6. Read the sentences and mark the one with 3 adjectives in it.

Ⓐ The pretty little lady was looking for her tiny kitten.
Ⓑ She lost her book and was very sad.
Ⓒ Don't play in the rain today.
Ⓓ We like our cupcakes very much.

7. Choose the correct adjective that will make the sentence correct. Mark your answer.
   The _____ pillow helped me sleep.

Ⓐ loudly
Ⓑ first-grade
Ⓒ fluffy
Ⓓ well

8. Choose the correct adjective for each sentence.

Sentence	Adjectives	correct adjective
We are _____ spellers.	well, good	
The _____ spider scared us.	always, huge	
The _____ bike was fun to ride.	very, orange	
My _____ sister let me go with her.	sweet, sweetly	

DAY 2

CHALLENGE YOURSELF!
✓ Add & Subtract Within 100 Using Place Values
✓ Adjectives and Adverbs

🌐 www.lumoslearning.com/a/dc2-37

See the first page for Signup details

1. Which equation with two addends will give you the same answer as the following equation with four addends?
   $42 + 11 + 14 + 9 = ?$

   Ⓐ $53 + 14 = ?$
   Ⓑ $23 + 11 = ?$
   Ⓒ $42 + 11 = ?$
   Ⓓ $53 + 23 = ?$

2. Which way is NOT another way you can add $21 + 24 + 55 + 2 = ?$

   Ⓐ $(21 + 24) + (55 + 2) = ?$
   Ⓑ $(21 + 2) + (55 + 24) = ?$
   Ⓒ $(2 + 24) + (55 + 21) = ?$
   Ⓓ $(21 + 55) + (21 + 2) = ?$

3. What is the sum of $43 + 54 + 20 + 5$?

4. Match each equation with its correct sum by placing a check mark under the correct column for each equation. Some columns might have more than one check, some columns might not have a check.

	110	121	111
28 + 17 + 44 + 22			
39 + 18 + 24 + 29			
6 + 68 + 12 + 25			

Context clues can be words or phrases in sentences that help you to understand what the meaning of the sentence is when you are reading.

Context clues are useful in understanding words that are spelled the same, sound the same, but have different meanings.

5. Read the sentences below. Highlight the words that are spelled and sound the same but have different meanings In each pair of sentences.

He broke his big toe.

She spent her money and was broke now.

The iron nail was rusty.

Mom will iron Dad's shirt.

The cave was dark.

The rain made the roof cave in.

6. Read the words and sentences. Choose the word that will make sense. Be careful as some words sound the same but are spelled differently and mean different things. Other words are spelled the same but have different meanings when used. Write the words in the blanks that belong. A word can be used more than one time.

mind
flower
flour
handle
stare

1. The handle of the milk jug was slippery.	
2. I always mind my parents.	
3. She did not stare at the strange looking car.	
4. What kind of flower is your favorite?	
5. What's on your mind?	
6. You need to use flour when you make a cake.	

7. Some words are rhyming words. Read the words and write them to their rhyming words in the blank.

about, relieve, ring, box

sing _____
fox _____
believe _____
scout _____

8. Read the words below. Highlight the two words in each row that sound the same but mean something different.

pies piece peace
knows nose knew

DAY 3

CHALLENGE YOURSELF!
✔ Add Four Two-digit Numbers
✔ The Context Clue

 www.lumoslearning.com/a/dc2-38

See the first page for Signup details

1. What is the value of x in the equation 109 + x = 309?

Ⓐ 481
Ⓑ 200
Ⓒ 208
Ⓓ 408

2. What is the value of x in the equation 385 − x = 300.

Ⓐ 685
Ⓑ 680
Ⓒ 0
Ⓓ 85

3. What is the difference between 825 and 399?

4. Match each equation with its correct sum or difference by placing a check mark under the correct column for each equation. Some columns might have more than one check, some columns might not have a check.

	313	303	302	312
124 + 179				
572 - 259				
491 - 189				
209 + 103				

Root words are main words. If letters are added to a root word, it becomes a new word. An example: help + ful = helpful.

5. Part A
Read the sentences and decide which is the best definition of the underlined word. The students need <u>additional</u> time to finish their work.

Ⓐ less
Ⓑ excellent
Ⓒ larger
Ⓓ more

Part B
We were <u>thankful</u> that our cat was not hurt.

Ⓐ full of thanks
Ⓑ not happy
Ⓒ full of regret
Ⓓ very sad

Part C
It was <u>thoughtful</u> of her to help the elderly lady.

Ⓐ rude
Ⓑ kind
Ⓒ useless
Ⓓ not important

6. Make new words by adding the ending to the root word. Write your answers.

care + ful =	
hope + less =	
break + able =	
thank + ful =	

7. Read the words and decide which endings were added to make the new words. Write the ending next to each word.

comfortable = _____

hopeless = _____

respectful = _____

playful = _____

8. Read the words in the box and write the correct root word for each of them.

Word	Word	Word	Root word
respectful	respected	respects	
careless	careful	caring	
playful	played	playing	
breakable	breaking	breaks	

DAY 4

CHALLENGE YOURSELF!
✔ Add And Subtract Within 1000
✔ Roots And Affixes

🌐 www.lumoslearning.com/a/dc2-39

See the first page for Signup details

1. Which statement is true?

   Ⓐ   399 is 10 more than 299.
   Ⓑ   418 is 10 less than 408.
   Ⓒ   977 is 100 more than 877.
   Ⓓ   208 is 10 more than 218.

2. Select all of the true statements below.

   Ⓐ   877 is 10 less than 887.
   Ⓑ   480 is 100 less than 380.
   Ⓒ   763 is 10 more than 663.
   Ⓓ   111 is 100 less than 211.
   Ⓔ   689 is 10 more than 699.

3. What number is 10 more than 999?

4. Place a check mark under each column that make the statements true.

	10 more	10 less	100 more	100 less
546 is ___ than 536				
297 is ___ than 397				
891 is ___ than 901				
1000 is ___ than 900				

Compound words are made by joining two words to make a new word.

5. Read the words and write the compound words next to them.

ham + burger =	
pop + corn =	
milk + shake =	
butter + fly =	
tooth + brush =	

6. Read the list of words and make new compound words from other words in the list. Write them in ABC order.

ball, bell, home, end, foot, work, week, door

7. Read the sentences and highlight the compound word in each sentence.

A. Chloe loves to go horseback riding.

B. Sam got a new skateboard!

C. What is wrong with Grandma?

D. Someone found my lost dog.

E. Watermelon is my favorite dessert.

8. Which compound word would be used if I am talking about something I carry my books in? Mark your answer.

Ⓐ firewood
Ⓑ snowman
Ⓒ backpack
Ⓓ cupcake

DAY 5

CHALLENGE YOURSELF!
✔ Mental Addition & Subtraction In Steps Of 10
✔ Connecting Related Words

 www.lumoslearning.com/a/dc2-40

See the first page
for Signup details

WEEK 9
SUMMER PRACTICE

BUNDLE OF TENS

1. Which choice represents 213?

Ⓐ

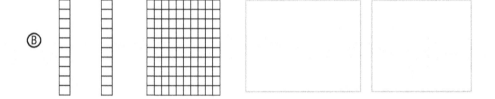

Ⓑ

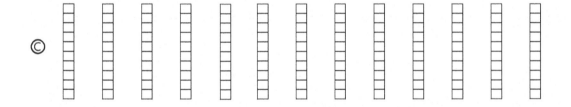

Ⓒ

Ⓓ

2. Choose the choice that the blocks below represent.

Ⓐ   7 hundreds, 1 ten, 2 ones
Ⓑ   7 tens , 2 hundreds, 1 one
Ⓒ   1 hundred, 2 ones, 7 tens
Ⓓ   2 hundreds, 7 tens, 2 ones

3. What number is represented by the blocks?

4. Place a check under the correct column to tell whether the number is less than 300 or more than 300.

	Less than 300	More than 300
13 tens, 200 ones		
14 tens, 150 ones		
27 tens, 3 ones		
15 ones, 20 tens		

Words can be related to each other in their meaning. Some words can be weaker or stronger than others. Example: big, gigantic would be in order from weaker to stronger.

5. Read the words below. Put them in the box in order from weaker to stronger meaning.

frightened
afraid

Weaker	Stronger

6. Choose the words that describe more than the underlined words in the sentences. Write them in the blanks.

frightened
awful
gorgeous
gigantic

a. Their dresses were <u>very pretty.</u>

b. Madeline was <u>very scared</u> when she saw the lion.

c. The spoiled milk tasted <u>very bad.</u>

d. The elephant was <u>very big.</u>

7. Read the words and sentences below. Write the correct antonym for the underlined words.

closed
yes
play
there

1. She said <u>no</u> to her mother.	
2. They wanted to <u>work</u>.	
3. The door was <u>open</u>.	
4. We were <u>here</u> when it started to rain.	

8. Some words that help us to read and write are opposites of other words. They are called antonyms. Read the words below and match them to their antonyms.

short	**tall**
happy	
left	
fast	
on	
hot	

(cold, sad, slow, right, off)

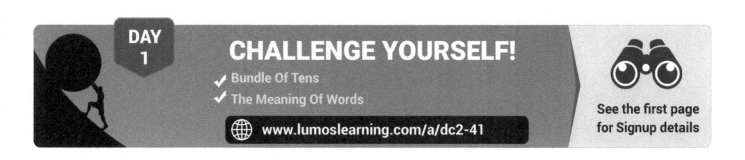

1. Lucy drew a line that was 7 inches. Select all of the possible representations of Lucy's line.

Ⓐ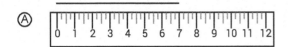

Ⓑ

Ⓒ

Ⓓ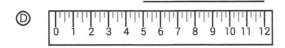

Ⓔ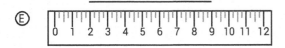

2. Travis cut a piece of ribbon that was 9 cm long. Which one of the following choices could be where Travis placed the ribbon on the ruler?

Ⓐ Travis' ribbon began on 3 cm and ended on 9 cm
Ⓑ Travis' ribbon began on 1 cm and ended on 9 cm
Ⓒ Travis' ribbon ended on 14 cm and began on 5 cm
Ⓓ Travis' ribbon ended on 19 cm and began on 27 cm

3. Kaylie placed her pencil on the ruler starting at 3 cm. If her pencil is 14 cm long, what number did Kaylie's pencil end on?

4. Match each line on the ruler with its length in inches.

	7 inches	2 inches	5 inches	9 inches
0 1 2 3 4 5 6 7 8 9 10 11 12				
0 1 2 3 4 5 6 7 8 9 10 11 12				
0 1 2 3 4 5 6 7 8 9 10 11 12				
0 1 2 3 4 5 6 7 8 9 10 11 12				

5. We use or think of words that tell about real-life things that we know or happen to us. Read the words, then match them to the clue words in the box.

	bright, colorful half-circle in the sky, pot of gold	baby dog, cute 4-legged pet	desktop, laptop, technology tool	buddy, pal, companion
friend				
computer				
puppy				
rainbow				

6. Read the words and sentences below. Choose the word that would best fit in the blank, given the real-life clues after each sentence. Use each word only one time.

(shout, recess, laugh, playground)

a. Most of the kids go to the _____ on Saturday to have fun. CLUE: slide, swing, equipment

b. He would _____ so loud at the jokes, his face would turn red. CLUE: chuckle, giggle

c. Jeff's favorite thing at school is _____. CLUE: friends, play, outside, games

d. My ears hurt every time I hear her _____! CLUE: scream, yell, holler

7. Some words fall into categories (real-life groups) of things we know well. Read the words and mark the best categories. Mark only 1 category for each word.

	Farm Animals	Indoor Pet Animals	Wild or Jungle Animals
cow			
dog			
horse			
elephant			
chicken			
lion			
hamster			
giraffe			
bear			

8. Read the words below and choose the ones that describe a stuffed animal. Mark your answer.

Ⓐ hard, prickly, rough
Ⓑ soft, cuddly, huggable

DAY 2

CHALLENGE YOURSELF!

✔ Measuring Length Of Objects
✔ Usage Of Words

🌐 www.lumoslearning.com/a/dc2-42

See the first page
for Signup details

1. **Look at the line on the ruler below. Choose the statement that correctly describes the measurement.**

Ⓐ   The line is 8 inches long.
Ⓑ   The line is 8 centimeters long.
Ⓒ   The line is 3 inches long.
Ⓓ   The line is 3 ½ inches long.

2. **Look at the line on the ruler below. Choose the true statement.**

Ⓐ   The line is about 3 inches.
Ⓑ   The line is about 3 centimeters.
Ⓒ   The line is close to 8 inches.
Ⓓ   The line is shorter than 4 centimeters.

3. **Kylie had a pencil that was 10 centimeters. She sharpened it and now it is 8 centimeters. How many centimeters were taken off when Kylie sharpened her pencil?**

4. **Look at the ruler below. Then match each statement as true or false by placing a check-mark under each column.**

	True	False
9 centimeters is shorter than 3 ½ inches		
4 ½ inches is between 11 and 12 centimeters		
5 inches is closer to 13 centimeters than 12 centimeters		

5. Verbs describe actions. The list below has verbs in it that are similar (related) to each other. Choose the verbs that would describe what you could do with a ball. Mark your answer.

Ⓐ eat, drink, smack, drool, sip, slurp
Ⓑ toss, drop, throw, hurl, pitch, bounce

6. Read the list of related verbs and match them to another verb that is like them in the box.

chat, talk	
tired, drowsy	
weep, sob	
tidy, clean	

(neat, cry, sleepy, speak)

7. Read the sentence below. Find the adjective that is related to good and write it.
The boys did an excellent job on their project.

8. Read the sentences below. Mark the one that uses a verb related to laugh.

Ⓐ They cried when the puppy was hurt.
Ⓑ She giggled when she saw the funny face on the clown.
Ⓒ He wanted to slurp his drink.
Ⓓ The teacher was happy with the good work her class did

DAY
3

CHALLENGE YOURSELF!
✔ Measure Length Of Object Using Two Different Length Units
✔ Shades Of Word Meaning

 www.lumoslearning.com/a/dc2-43

See the first page
for Signup details

1. The length of a sheet of paper is about 18 _____?

- Ⓐ Centimeters
- Ⓑ Feet
- Ⓒ Inches
- Ⓓ Meters

2. The height of a refrigerator is about 2 ___?

- Ⓐ Centimeters
- Ⓑ Feet
- Ⓒ Inches
- Ⓓ Meters

3. Angelica <u>correctly</u> answered the question "About how many inches is a ruler?" What number did Angelica say?

4. Complete the table by filling in the unit that is the best estimate for each row.

	Centimeter	Feet	Inches	Meters
The height of a birthday candle is about 2 __?				
The height of a chair is about 1 __?				
The height of a box of cereal is about 12 __?				
The height of a vacuum cleaner is about 4 __?				

Read the conversation below. Answer the questions about the words. Remember that adjectives describe nouns, verbs tell action, and adverbs help the verb.

George <u>said</u>, "Let's go on a hike in the <u>deep</u> woods today!"

"No way!" <u>shouted</u> Timothy. "I am <u>frightened</u> of the <u>dark</u> woods."

"Don't be <u>scared</u>!" George <u>replied</u>. "We'll take my <u>guard</u> dog with us. Smokey is a <u>great watch</u> dog. He will keep us safe from <u>harm</u>."

1. Which words describe the woods? Write them.

2. Which words tell about being afraid? Write them.

3. Which words below tell how George and Timothy talked? Mark 3 words from the story.

- Ⓐ answered
- Ⓑ spoke
- Ⓒ replied
- Ⓓ said
- Ⓔ shouted

4. Use the words below and write a conversation between you and a friend. Be sure to use quotation marks, capital letters, and punctuation correctly.

bright sunlight

wonderful playground

joyfully swinging

LumosLearning.com

1. Choose the correct comparison about Rectangle A and B below

Rectangle A

Rectangle B

Ⓐ Rectangle A is 1 inch longer than Rectangle B.
Ⓑ Rectangle A is ½ centimeter longer than Rectangle B.
Ⓒ Rectangle B is ½ inch shorter than Rectangle A.
Ⓓ Rectangle B is 1 inch shorter than Rectangle B.

2. Choose the correct comparison about Rectangle A and B below.

Rectangle A

Rectangle B

Ⓐ Rectangle B is 4 inches longer than Rectangle A.
Ⓑ Rectangle A is 4 cm shorter than Rectangle B.
Ⓒ Rectangle A is 8 cm shorter than Rectangle B.
Ⓓ Rectangle B is 12 inches longer than Rectangle A.

3. How many inches longer is Rectangle A than Rectangle B.

Rectangle A

Rectangle B

4. Bubble in the circle under the correct statement for each row.

	Line A is 6 cm shorter than Line B.	Line A and Line B are the same length.	Line A is 1 inch longer than Line B.	Line B is 4 inches shorter than Line A.
Line A / Line B with ruler	○	○	○	○
Line A / Line B with ruler	○	○	○	○
Line A / Line B with ruler	○	○	○	○
Line A / Line B with ruler	○	○	○	○

Informative/Explanatory Writing

You read information about many things. When we write or read passages that tell or inform us, we call it informative, or explanatory writing. Your science and social studies books have this kind of writing.

Informative writing includes a topic sentence that tells what you are about to read. Then important facts are given to tell you more. These facts give examples to support them. At the end of the writing, there is a concluding statement that retells the topic sentence.

5. What does an informative/explanatory piece of writing tell you? Mark the best answer.

- Ⓐ It gives you examples.
- Ⓑ It has a topic sentence.
- Ⓒ It has a conclusion.
- Ⓓ It tells or informs you about things.

Read the information below and answer the question no 2, 3 & 4.

Spring

We see weather changes along with new animal and plant life in the Spring.
Spring is a season that comes after winter and before summer. The weather is not as cold as in winter.

The sun rises earlier in the morning and sets later in the afternoon during Spring. The months when Spring occurs in the U.S. are March through May.

Flowers bloom in Spring and trees have new leaves. Many people grow flowers and vegetables during this season.

Animals also have babies during Spring. Birds and rabbits can be seen more outside.

6. Which is the topic sentence in the writing?

- Ⓐ The months when Spring occurs in the U.S. are March through May.
- Ⓑ We see weather changes along with new animal and plant life in the Spring.
- Ⓒ Many people grow flowers and vegetables during this season.
- Ⓓ Flowers bloom in Spring and trees have new leaves.

7. **What are the 3 facts that are used in the writing about Spring?**

Ⓐ Animals have babies
Ⓑ School is out
Ⓒ Dogs bark
Ⓓ Flowers bloom and leaves grow
Ⓔ Weather is cooler

8. **The writing does not have a concluding statement. Choose the sentence that would best help to end this writing about Spring.**

Ⓐ Spring has weather changes.
Ⓑ Leaves come out.
Ⓒ Baby birds are born
Ⓓ Spring brings cooler weather and new life for animals and plants.

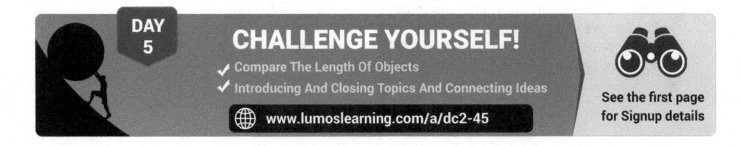

DAY 5

CHALLENGE YOURSELF!
✔ Compare The Length Of Objects
✔ Introducing And Closing Topics And Connecting Ideas

www.lumoslearning.com/a/dc2-45

See the first page
for Signup details

WEEK 10
LUMOS SHORT STORY & PHOTO CONTEST 2025

Write a short story based on your summer experiences and get a chance to win **$100 cash prize + 1 year free subscription to Lumos StepUp + trophy with a certificate**.

To enter the competition follow the instructions.

STEP 1

↓

Visit
www.lumoslearning.com/a/grade2
to register for online fun summer
program.

STEP 2

↓

After registering, you can log
in to your account and enter
your summer story in Week
10 under "**Lumos Short Story
Competition 2025**"

Note: If you have already registered, you can simply log in to your account and submit the story for the competition.

Last date for submission is August 31, 2025

WEEKLY FUN SUMMER PHOTO CONTEST

Take a picture of your summer fun activity and share it on Twitter or Instagram

Use the #SummerLearning mention

@LumosLearning on
Twitter

@lumos.learning on
Instagram

Tag friends and increase your chances of winning the contest.

PARTICIPATE AND STAND A CHANCE TO WIN $50 AMAZON GIFT CARD!

2024 Winning Story

"This summer before my seventh grade, I embarked on an unforgettable trip to China. The scorching sun marked the beginning of an exciting adventure in a new country, where I anticipated the heat, walked until my feet ached, and most importantly, created enduring memories.

I eagerly welcomed the morning sun, commencing my days between 7 and 8 a.m., occasionally rising at 5 a.m. during my stay at my Aunt Sandy and Uncle Danny's place. I treasured the time I spent visiting my grandparents and receiving loving attention from my uncles, aunts, and cousins. Being the youngest among them, I forged strong connections. I have two main cousins and a few second cousins, and sometimes I consider my dad's best friends' kids as my own, which feels slightly unfamiliar. This marked my first visit to China, having lived in Canada my entire life.

I still vividly remember the delightful days filled with dining at elegant restaurants and the joy of online shopping for unique items that caught my eye. Our explorations took us on an incredible journey to vibrant cities like Beijing and Xi'an, where we immersed ourselves in the rich cultural heritage and historical wonders of China.

During our memorable visit to Xi'an (northern west China), the sheer magnificence of the Terracotta Warriors in all three pits left us in awe. Witnessing the remarkably preserved seven intact ones was truly an unforgettable experience that we will always cherish. As if this wasn't enough, we had the opportunity to try hand crafting mini Terracotta Warriors at a local sculpting school. Although our creations unfortunately couldn't withstand the test of time and weather, the experience was incredible, and we gained a newfound appreciation for the skill and artistry involved in creating these ancient wonders.

The high speed train (365 km/hr) journey to Beijing (China's capital) was an adventure in itself, offering breathtaking views and creating countless cherished memories. The city's impressive architecture, blending with ancient traditions with modern innovations, left an awestruck impression on us. Exploring the bustling streets and admiring the iconic landmarks, such as the Forbidden City (why is it called the Forbidden City if we can go in it?) and the Summer Palace (was it made in the summer?), allowed us to immerse ourselves in the rich history and vibrant culture of China.

Of course, no trip to China would be complete without a visit to the Great Wall. Despite the limited time due to our tour group's schedule, the exhilaration of walking along this ancient marvel filled our hearts with immense joy and a profound sense of awe. The magnitude of the wall and the stunning views reminded us of the enduring legacy of this architectural masterpiece.

Looking back, my trip to China was nothing short of a dream come true, and the memories of that adventure still bring a smile to my face. Reflecting on our journey, we are filled with gratitude for the opportunity to witness the wonders of China and to immerse ourselves in its rich tapestry of history and culture.

Student Name: Erin Zhu
Grade: 7

FOR ACCESS TO ANSWER KEY & DETAILED EXPLANATIONS

Visit: *lumoslearning.com/a/g2a*

or Scan the QR code

Why are Answer Keys Digital?

At Lumos Learning, we care about your learning and the environment! That's why, instead of adding extra pages for the answer key and explanations, we've made them available digitally.

By doing this, we are saving **more than 50 pages per book!** This small change would save **over 2.5 million pages**.

Every small action counts! By choosing digital access, **you are helping** reduce waste and protect our planet for the future.

Environmental Impact

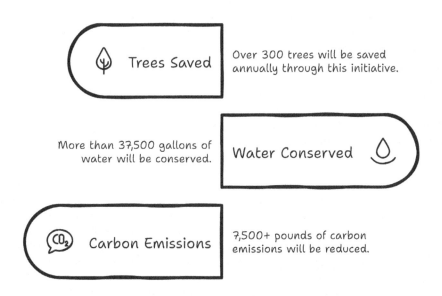

Trees Saved — Over 300 trees will be saved annually through this initiative.

More than 37,500 gallons of water will be conserved. — Water Conserved

Carbon Emissions — 7,500+ pounds of carbon emissions will be reduced.

Lumos tedBooks for State Test Practice

Lumos tedBook for standardized test practice provides necessary grade-specific state assessment practice and skills mastery. Each tedBook includes hundreds of standards-aligned practice questions and online summative assessments that mirror actual state tests.

The workbook provides students access to thousands of valuable learning resources such as worksheets, videos, apps, books, and much more.

Lumos Learning tedBooks for State Assessment	
Smarter Balanced Math & ELA Practice Book	AK STAR Math & ELA Practice Book
ACAP Math & ELA Practice Book	ISASP Math & ELA Practice Book
NJSLA Math & ELA Practice Book	ISAT Math & ELA Practice Book
ATLAS Math & ELA Practice Book	M-STEP Math & ELA Practice Book
IAR Math & ELA Practice Book	MAST Math & ELA Practice Book
FAST Math & ELA Practice Book	MECAS Math & ELA Practice Book
GMAS Math & ELA Practice Book	ND A+ Math & ELA Practice Book
NYST Math & ELA Practice Book	NH SAS Math & ELA Practice Book
ILEARN Math & ELA Practice Book	OSAS Math & ELA Practice Book
LEAP Math & ELA Practice Book	RICAS Math & ELA Practice Book
MAP Math & ELA Practice Book	VTCAP Math & ELA Practice Book
MAAP Math & ELA Practice Book	WFE Math & ELA Practice Book
AASA Math & ELA Practice Book	WVGSA Math & ELA Practice Book
MCAP Math & ELA Practice Book	WYTOPP Math & ELA Practice Book
OST Math & ELA Practice Book	
MCAS Math & ELA Practice Book	
CMAS Math & ELA Practice Book	
TCAP Math & ELA Practice Book	
STAAR Math & RLA Practice Book	
NM-MSSA Math & ELA Practice Book	
KSA Math & ELA Practice Book	
KAP Math & ELA Practice Book	
OSTP Math & ELA Practice Book	

Buy Now At Leading Book Stores

www.lumoslearning.com/a/lumostedbooks

Made in USA - Kendallville, IN
86985_9781097418343
05.06.2025 2045